Praise for *The 4 Habits of Joy-Filled People*

Marcus Warner and Chris Coursey have hit the jackpot with this new book. We all live in a world that is filled with fears and problems, but this book shares how to find joy in the midst of difficult circumstances. What has been missing until recent years is how our brains work—how the brain is "wired" to process negative emotions and return to joy. Their fascinating, and eminently readable book shares clear pathways that can be developed, resulting in the transformation we seek to return to joy. I can't think of anyone who doesn't need it!

BILL ATWOOD
Author of numerous books on applied neuroscience, including The General, The Boy, *and* Recapturing Joy

In *The 4 Habits of Joy-Filled People*, Marcus and Chris have captured the essence of our time by showcasing the significance of why knowing and living joy is critical for humanity to exist and survive. They point out through in-depth research and powerful stories that we all crave this good feeling because we are scientifically and spiritually WIRED to live a life of joy. The joy workouts and techniques carefully outlined give generations to come hope. The hope is that each of us can be seen and heard through the building of our own joy house, and that ultimately we will make decisions with the confidence and courage that is developed through these principles. I believe that this book will have a profound impact on how we create success in life, and this newfound success will lead to more peace and calm for all. *The 4 Habits of Joy-Filled People* was a delightful read, easy to consume, and fun to implement! Brilliant!

SHERYL LYNN
Visionary and founder, JOYELY, LLC; Chair of Joy™ Experience

This book has transformed how I view my life, my kids, my marriage. I wish everyone could learn these super practical skills that are forward facing; they work toward living the life you want to live and feeling the way you want to feel instead of so many approaches that backfire because they focus on negativity. Chris and Marcus take the science of attachment and joy, integrate it with a mind-body approach and boil it down into simple, effective life changing habits that everyone can use to live their best life. A lot of people might say that you can't change how you feel, but this book doesn't just tell you that you can, it shows you how to do it. The simple skills of practicing appreciation and learning to calm your body are game-changing. And these guys teach you how to do it.

EMMA MCADAM
LMFT, Creator of Therapy in a Nutshell

Above all emotions, JOY has a unique life-impacting role in creating and sustaining healthy mental well-being and connecting relationships. Marcus Warner takes this complicated reality and simplifies it masterfully for practical daily application. Beyond spiritual understanding, appropriating joy despite circumstances provides one of life's most foundational skills to learn and impart. As parents of a dozen children, raising joy-filled lives has provided the glue for their fulfilled families. This book provides all the elements to make that possible!

BILL & PAMELA MUTZ
FamilyLife Weekend to Remember Speakers

Marcus Warner and Chris Coursey are trusted guides on the journey I am on to becoming more fully human. My life is being transformed by the countercultural message of this book. I wish I had known these things thirty years ago, and I can't wait to share this book with my children, grandchildren, and friends.

RAY WOOLRIDGE
Former US Army Brigadier General, Executive Director of Life Model Works, and the coauthor of Escaping Enemy Mode: How Our Brains Unite or Divide Us

The 4 Habits of
Joy-Filled People

*15-Minute Brain Science Hacks
to a More Connected and Satisfying Life*

Marcus Warner *and* Chris M. Coursey

NORTHFIELD PUBLISHING

CHICAGO

Scripture quotations marked CSB have been taken from the Christian Standard Bible®, Copyright © 2017 by Holman Bible Publishers. Used by permission. Christian Standard Bible® and CSB® are federally registered trademarks of Holman Bible Publishers.

Scripture quotations marked (NIV) are taken from the Holy Bible, New International Version®, NIV®. Copyright © 1973, 1978, 1984, 2011 by Biblica, Inc.™ Used by permission of Zondervan. All rights reserved worldwide. www.zondervan.com The "NIV" and "New International Version" are trademarks registered in the United States Patent and Trademark Office by Biblica, Inc.™

Some names and identifying details have been changed to protect the privacy of individuals.

Edited by Elizabeth Cody Newenhuyse
Interior and cover design: Erik M. Peterson
Cover illustration of fingerprint copyright © 2022 by allapen/Adobe Stock (41998652). All rights reserved.
Cover illustration of watercolor tree copyright © 2022 by DesignToonsy/Adobe Stock (424840317). All rights reserved.
Chris M. Coursey photo: Charles Spoelstra

Library of Congress Cataloging-in-Publication Data

Names: Warner, Marcus, author. | Coursey, Chris, author.
Title: The 4 habits of joy-filled people : 15 minute brain science hacks to a more connected and satisfying life / Marcus Warner and Chris M. Coursey.
Other titles: Four habits of joy-filled people
Description: Chicago : Northfield Publishing, 2023. | Includes bibliographical references. | Summary: "Joy is possible. The authors show how to build habits that fill our lives with joy and satisfaction. Based on the latest neuroscience and attachment theory-but written in everyday language-this book is easy to comprehend. The authors provide exercises and tools you can put into practice immediately"-- Provided by publisher.
Identifiers: LCCN 2022051276 (print) | LCCN 2022051277 (ebook) | ISBN 9780802431394 (paperback) | ISBN 9780802473264 (ebook)
Subjects: LCSH: Joy. | Conduct of life.
Classification: LCC BF575.H27 W365 2023 (print) | LCC BF575.H27 (ebook) | DDC 158--dc23/eng/20221212
LC record available at https://lccn.loc.gov/2022051276
LC ebook record available at https://lccn.loc.gov/2022051277

We hope you enjoy this book from Northfield Publishing. Our goal is to provide high-quality, thought-provoking books and products that connect truth to your real needs and challenges. For more information on other books and products that will help you with all your important relationships, go to northfieldpublishing.com or write to:

Northfield Publishing
820 N. LaSalle Boulevard
Chicago, IL 60610

1 3 5 7 9 10 8 6 4 2

Printed in the United States of America

We dedicate this book to Jim Wilder
for his significant role in opening our eyes
to the power of joy and how crucial it is to life.

CONTENTS

INTRODUCTION

IF YOU ARE LIKE US, you didn't grow up thinking of joy as a high priority. It may have seemed like something random that happened every now and then, but we certainly wouldn't have called it the fuel of life. It was much more like the icing on the cake of life—something that you might get to experience only after the basics of life were taken care of. But what we are learning from neuroscience is that joy is not a luxury. It is a necessity. Without joy, our brains will default to running on fear. As we will see, that is a major problem at several levels.

Consider just a few reasons why joy is so important:

- Joy is awesome! Joy is a high-energy feeling that you can't wait to share with others. It motivates us to be with the people we love, and we feel alive and on top of the world when joy is present in our interactions. Joy gives us energy, hope, and the ability to express our love. Joy is what brings us together and invigorates us to look forward to our day.

Just think about someone you enjoy and reflect on how you feel when you are with this person—that's joy!

- The alternative to joy is fear, and a fear-fueled brain is not a pretty thing. When fear runs our brain, we learn to "fear map" our world. We amplify pain and live waiting for the other shoe to drop. When our brain learns to run on joy, we still have problems to solve, but our brain becomes trained to understand that problems aren't the end of the world. As long as my brain knows it can get back to a place of peace, it will naturally be less anxious. We don't fret when the sun is setting because we know it will return in the morning.

- Joy helps you endure hardship well. Joy gives us the strength to deal with emotional pain. The idea of living with joy doesn't mean that we don't suffer or feel emotional pain. It doesn't even mean that we get past our emotional pain quickly. It means that despite the emotional pain we have, we can still find relational joy in the midst of the hard stuff. For example, joy-filled people still grieve when they lose a loved one. The point is not that

> *The alternative to joy is fear, and a fear-fueled brain is not a pretty thing.*

joy makes them immune to bad feelings. The point is that even in the midst of the upsetting emotions, they can share joy with others, and that joy helps them get through the hard times.

- Low levels of joy make us vulnerable to artificial substitutes for the real thing. Addictions form as attachments to non-relational stimulants that usually create a sense of pleasure or momentary happiness. Thus, my addiction makes me feel happy temporarily. It gives me a short-term pleasure boost that numbs my pain and replaces it with pleasure. The problem, of course, is that it doesn't last and it creates other problems that generally make my life worse than if I didn't have the addiction.

- Joy makes us healthier people. More and more research is supporting what we have likely already suspected. Just as stress is harmful to our physical health, so happiness—especially relational happiness, which is what we call joy—has a positive effect. Stress expert Dr. Andrew Steptoe of University College in London states that while stress has a negative effect on certain biological systems, happiness "has a protective effect on these same biological pathways."[1] We now know that simply thinking about joy and reflecting on the "good stuff" changes enzymes in our body, and these changes help prevent inflammatory disease.[2]

What research is revealing is that the brain is uniquely tuned to crave joy. Nothing provides greater motivation than this high-octane fuel. The good news is that we can train our brains to transition from living on the fuel of fear to living on the fuel of joy. If you find yourself too often running on fear and not experiencing enough joy to get you through the tough stuff, this book can be your road map to greater emotional stability and resilience.

CHAPTER 1

Joy, Trauma, and Building Our House

I'LL NEVER FORGET SITTING in the county jail feeling like my life was over. I (Chris) was in college and had been pulled over with my second DUI in only a year. I thought of myself as a fun guy. People liked hanging out with me. I certainly loved going to parties, but in that moment of darkness came a growing clarity—my life wasn't working. Something needed to change. Sitting in the county lockup that night, I never dreamed that someday I would become a relationship expert who trained people on how to live with joy.

As part of the sentence for my DUIs I had to give up my license, seek counseling, and pay hefty fines. Without a license to drive, I was limited on my options, so that summer I joined an out-of-state ministry for a summer internship. I found myself at a center that helped severely traumatized people. Talk about a fish out of water! This was the last place I wanted to be. I was away from all my friends, away from any sign of familiarity. I wanted to put in my time and get out of there as quickly as I could. Just a few days into the internship, I decided it was time to leave. However, this organization was run by Christians and, before I could leave, I knew they would ask if I had prayed about my decision. I wanted to give them an honest answer, so I prayed. I said, "God, if I'm supposed to be here, please show me, otherwise I'm leaving in the morning."

Within a few minutes, I realized there was a new thought bouncing around in my head like a Ping-Pong ball. The thought made no sense to me, but I kept seeing the words floating in my mind. It was simply the words, "Isaiah 61." Now, I had grown up in church but had not taken my faith very seriously up to this point. It occurred to me that Isaiah sounded like a book in the Bible. I found a Bible on the shelf where I was staying, and looked for the table of contents. Sure enough, there was an Isaiah about two-thirds of the way down the list of books. I then thought, "What are the odds that Isaiah has sixty-one chapters?" I flipped through the pages and was completely shocked to find that there was indeed an Isaiah 61. The next words I read changed my life. It said, "The Spirit of the Sovereign LORD is on me, because the LORD has anointed me to proclaim good news to the poor. He has sent me to bind up the brokenhearted, to proclaim freedom for the captives and release from darkness for the prisoners" (v. 1 NIV). In that moment of insight, I realized that I was right where I was supposed to be. I felt like God wanted me to walk alongside deeply wounded people—to do something to bind up their broken hearts and help them find freedom from the prisons of mental darkness in which so many of them lived.

It was this unexpected calling to work with highly traumatized people that led me to neuroscience, attachment theory, and the importance of joy.

TWO LIFE-CHANGING RELATIONSHIPS

While working at this center, I made two life-changing relationships. First, after a few years of working there, I met my future wife, Jen. She arrived as a volunteer, and we found ourselves working together more and more often. Like me, Jen was overcoming some issues in her own life. She often struggled with depression so debilitating it kept her from getting out of bed. Gradually, we both realized that our joy levels increased as we spent time together. We became friends. We eventually fell in love and got married.

The second life-changing relationship was with Dr. Jim Wilder. I heard Jim speak at conferences, and several times he came to visit our center as a guest to help us understand the brain and attachment theory. It was Dr. Wilder who introduced us to the importance of joy.

Both Jen and I were highly motivated to apply what Dr. Wilder was teaching. We wanted more than that, however. We wanted to figure out how to make this material as practical as possible for the people we were trying to help. Over time, Dr. Wilder would suggest practices we could use to help those we served—practical steps and exercises based on brain science. While I tested these training methods, my colleagues and I would discuss what worked and what didn't. I would report back to Jim the effects of this training. Within a short time Jim and I were running training events called THRIVE Training, and Jen counted nineteen skills in our training that were essential to helping people grow their emotional capacity. I (Chris) gained experience in creating exercises to help people grow missing relational skills.

A TRAUMA AND B TRAUMA

The core issue we were trying to address was how to help adults learn relational and emotional skills they should have developed as children. In his model, Dr. Wilder taught that two kinds of traumas had stunted the emotional development of our clients.[1] Along the way, we discovered that everybody has some level of stunted maturity because of these two kinds of trauma. Jim called these A Trauma and B Trauma.

Most of us are familiar with B Trauma. B stands for the "bad" stuff that happens to us—like verbal, psychological, sexual, or physical abuse. B Trauma stunts our maturity because of the things that we've been through. All of the people we were trying to help at this center had gone through significant B Trauma. Some had been beaten, some sexually abused, some psychologically tormented. Some had even been tortured. It was easy to see how B Trauma impacted their lives.

Perhaps less familiar to many of us is what we know as A Trauma. A stands for the "absence" of the good stuff we all need. For example, if no one stayed relationally present with us as children while we recovered from big emotions like shame, anger, and fear, chances are high we never developed the skill to bounce back from these sometimes overwhelming emotions. As a result of missing these experiences, a hole began to form in our maturity. A Trauma includes things like neglect, not getting hugs, missing out on having both parents in the home, and basically any other good thing that would have helped us mature. A Trauma stunts our maturity development because of the good experiences we miss.

It sometimes helps to think of A Trauma this way. If you wanted to kill a plant, how would you do it? The most common answer we hear is, "Don't water it," followed by "don't give it the right amount of sunlight or the right kind of soil." Clearly, what you don't give a plant can kill it. And what you don't give to a child can kill their development.

The temptation at the ministry where Jen and I were working was to spend all our time trying to help with the B Trauma. However, what we discovered was that recovery was actually more predictable based on how well people overcame the A Trauma in their lives. As we spent more and more time helping people do the exercises that filled the holes left by A Trauma, we could see their joy levels increase noticeably. People with higher levels of joy had less trouble processing their B Trauma, while people with low joy levels and minimal life skills related to A Trauma often struggled to make any progress with getting past the B Trauma in their lives.

WE CAN ALL GROW OUR CAPACITY FOR JOY

The good news is that what Jen and I (Chris) learned about helping people overcome the A Trauma in their lives taught us lessons that anyone can learn, so that all of us can intentionally grow our capacity for joy. The four habits taught in this book serve as a summary of the foundational lessons that can move our default setting from fear to joy. Here are a few testimonies of people who went through the five-day training program we ran with Dr. Jim Wilder called THRIVE Training.[2]

Marvin, a professional, wrote us after his training week,

I have attended and participated in hundreds of seminars, conferences, and workshops over the timeline of my career. I have trained thousands of professionals through my private practice as a consultant. However, I have never been impacted in the manner in which I was through the THRIVE Training. This has changed my life forever. Daily, I am witnessing the impact of joy in the lives of the men I minister to as a result of THRIVE through what was deposited into my soul. THRIVE will remain a part of my continued growth and development for the rest of my life. Thank you so very much for such a memorable and life-changing experience and opportunity!

Julie wrote to share her experience and highlight some of the changes in her marriage after participating in THRIVE Training.

[Because of this training], I now know how to get and stay in joy. Thank you! It is almost too good to be true. Once you experience genuine joy, you cannot live without it.

Last, Gail wrote to express her observations about her pastor who returned from the THRIVE Training:

My pastor really gained something out of your training last week. He didn't just come back with information; he came back changed. And I think it's great. I've never seen something like this happen to him. It's like he's finally alive with joy, and really REALLY "there." Thank you for the work you are doing to spread relational skills!

We share these stories to let you know the habits you are about to learn can truly be life-changing. Just reading this book won't change anything, but putting into practice what you learn here can make all the difference in the world.

So, how do we grow our capacity for joy? Let's get started.

TEARING DOWN THE HOUSE OF FEAR

We all have an inner world. It is a world of thoughts, emotions, and impulses that others don't see. We can smile at people around us while we are dying inside. We can put on a good front even when inwardly we feel like we are falling apart. In order to grow our capacity for joy, we have to bring some structure to that inner world. We have to tear down the house of fear in which most of us live, and begin building a house of joy.

Joy is the key to emotional resilience. It is like the air in the ball that lets it bounce. Let's face it. No one goes to counseling because they have too much joy and need to get rid of some of it. We don't stand around the water cooler at the office and complain to our coworkers about all the joy we had over the weekend or whine about how joy is ruining our lives. When we start our day with joy, it is easier to face the challenges we will meet throughout the day. When we know we will end our day in a place of joy and peace, sleep comes more easily and we do not dread life quite so much. Knowing we can get back to a place of joy helps us bounce back from hard experiences.

So how do we build a joy house in our inner world?

First, we need a foundation. When it comes to joy, that foundation is laid by two essential habits—*calming* and *appreciation*. It has been said that the ability to share high-energy states like joy, then quiet and calm from upsetting emotions, is the number one predictor of emotional stability throughout life.[3] Nothing grows joy faster than learning to experience the feeling of appreciation several times a day. Routinely quieting ourselves and entering into feelings of appreciation just a few times each day lays a foundation for a life of joy as it trains our brains that joy and peace are normal experiences.

Once the foundation of calming and appreciation has been laid, our house needs to be framed. This framework helps us return to joy and peace from a variety of troubling emotions. To construct this part of our joy house, one of the most important habits we can form is that of *storytelling*. We are specifically referring to sharing brain-friendly "joy stories." These are practiced tales of times we faced upsetting emotions without getting overwhelmed, or times we got overwhelmed initially but were able to recover. Collecting such stories constructs a framework for resilience in our brains. "Joy stories" anchor our brains in the understanding that no matter what emotion I may be feeling right now, it is not the end of the world. There is a path back to joy from there.

After our foundation and framework are in place, it is time to finish the structure and complete our joy house.

We do this by learning to attack the toxic thinking that so often keeps us locked in negative, self-defeating emotions and behaviors. Many of us are imprisoned by unhelpful narratives about how unlovable we are, or what failures we are, or how the world is out to get us. As these narratives take root, toxic thinking becomes a habit of its own and we need a game plan for winning the battle for our minds.

Not only do we want to teach you the four habits that help you build your own joy house, we want to help you learn how to fill that house with good things that make life satisfying as opposed to the okay (or sometimes bad) things that fill our lives with meaninglessness and trouble. Learning to distinguish what is truly satisfying from what is temporarily pleasurable is essential to building a life worth living.

To help you remember the four habits you will need to build your joy house, we have outlined them to spell the word CASA. (It seemed appropriate for the model.) Here are the four habits of joy-filled people.

C—Calming (Learning to live with a quiet mind)
A—Appreciating (Learning to find joy in the everyday pleasures of life)
S—Storytelling (Developing a positive narrative of how to act like our best selves when facing upsetting emotions)
A—Attacking toxic thoughts (Creating a strategy for replacing thoughts that imprison us in unpleasant emotions)

In the chapters ahead we will explain why these habits are so important, give you some practical ideas for how to build these habits, and provide you with exercises to get you started. We want everyone we know to grow their capacity to live with joy.

BUSTING SOME MYTHS ABOUT JOY

It is not uncommon to think that high-joy people must have some unfair advantage over the rest of us. Perhaps they were simply born happy, or maybe their life is easier than ours. In Western cultures we also tend to see joy as a choice and we can beat ourselves up for not being better at choosing this happy emotion. As we try to understand the importance of joy, let's consider three common—and false—beliefs about joy.

Joy is a choice. While there are choices we can make that increase the odds of feeling joy, there is a simple fact that eliminates the idea that joy is a choice. Joy happens predominantly in the relational right hemisphere of the brain, while choices and cognition happen in the left. One of the reasons this is significant is that the data flow in the brain moves from right to left, not the other way around. Right-brain activity informs left-brain activity, not the reverse. We could take the rest of the book to explain how Western ideas regarding the will have influenced the way we look at everything from love and joy to character and destiny. Our point here is that joy is primarily a relational experience that is more like a reflex anchored in the relational part of our brain.

How can our choices help us move toward joy? Here are a few examples. We can choose to visit a friend who lights up to see us. We can choose to dwell on memories of relational joy. We can choose to spend time quieting and appreciating the good things in life. One of the more powerful stories we have heard about someone who made the choice to practice appreciation despite adverse circumstances involves a member of the Dutch Resistance during World War II. Her name was Betsie ten Boom. She and her sister, Corrie, were arrested for hiding Jews in their home and sent to a Nazi concentration camp. As you can imagine, there was very little about the camp to inspire joy. But Betsie made a choice. She decided to find something to appreciate in every situation she had to endure. Her demeanor and joyful attitude gave strength to others. She tried to teach her sister the importance of living this way—of giving thanks in everything. Corrie was a bit slower to pick up the habit.

One situation in particular stood out. She and her sister along with a crowd of other women were packed into inadequate barracks. Nothing about these conditions was appealing. To make matters worse, the place was infested with lice. Corrie hit her limit. She told Betsie, "There is no way I am thanking God for lice!" With Betsie's encouragement, Corrie begrudgingly made the choice to thank

God anyway, even though she couldn't see how in the world there could be anything good about lice.

Within a few weeks, Corrie and Betsie began to notice that the guards didn't like the lice, either. They stayed away from their barracks and largely left these women alone. As a result, every evening they were able to read from a smuggled Bible and encourage one another in prayer. Consequently, the morale in this group of women stayed relatively strong. They were able to strengthen one another in ways that gave them the joy and strength they needed to face the daily horror of the place. None of this would have been possible without the lice.[4]

Some people are just born joyful. Have you ever met someone and thought, "It seems like this person was just born happy"? I (Marcus) recently had the chance to work with a former executive at a large bank who exudes joy. She began her career as a teller and worked her way up to serving in a corporate leadership position with one of the largest banks in America. Part of her secret was that she was so good with people. Everyone liked spending time with her, and she was good at dealing with problems in a way that let people know they had been seen, heard, and appreciated. In talking to her about her optimistic, positive approach to life, she said that it just came naturally. She didn't remember ever thinking about why she did it or how to do it. The skills were just there. They showed up without her having to think about them.

For some of us, this would seem to suggest that she was simply born this way. But neuroscience points us in another direction. She had been raised in a large and basically happy family. She grew up with a lot of smiles, a lot of people who were happy to see her, and lots of family members who knew how to navigate troubling emotions well. As a result, the mirror neurons in her brain that learn by watching and imitating got lots of practice in learning how to live with joy and return to joy from upsetting situations. Many of these skills were likely already in place by the time she was three years old and just continued to develop with practice. Thus, by the time she was an adult, she had formed well-established habits that showed up without even having to think about them. This is how joy-fueled maturity formation is supposed to happen.

There is evidence that genetics and heredity play a role in predisposing people toward joy, so we see both nature and nurture have a role in how the brain grows and organizes itself over time.[5] However, at the time of birth the part of the brain that grows with the experience of joy is barely developed.[6] How well it develops and grows is largely influenced by relational activity.[7]

Our brains need to share joy with other people and learn how to return to joy from all of the various emotions that threaten to overwhelm us. The essential skills can be developed before we are even old enough to speak.[8]

Joy-filled people have fewer problems than low-joy people. You would think that the happiest people in the world would be those who are the richest, healthiest, and most influential. But that is rarely the case. History is replete with the stories of people who had it all and died miserable, lonely, and—in some cases—even took their own lives. On the other hand, the world is filled with people who struggle to make ends meet, have few opportunities for upward mobility, and even face persecution, but live with joy. I (Marcus) formerly served on the board of an organization that ran "mercy homes" and training centers throughout India. The Mercy Homes were something like orphanages. They took in people who had lost their families. They also provided training for low-income people and helped them start microbusinesses. Eventually, this organization was able to open a hospital just in time to help with the COVID crisis.

I had the privilege of traveling to India and participating in the ribbon-cutting ceremony that opened their primary training center. Having grown up in northern Indiana, India was quite a culture shock for me.

> *The world is filled with people who struggle to make ends meet, have few opportunities for upward mobility, and even face persecution, but live with joy.*

I had never seen so many people living in poverty. The sheer magnitude of the problem is overwhelming. In the midst of a country in which over 600 million people live in poverty, it was equally striking to see the joy with which the people in the Mercy Homes lived. These were people who had lost everything, but you couldn't help but leave encouraged and uplifted after spending time with them. I have encountered similar situations in a variety of countries I have visited—low-income people with very hard lives who live with more joy than most well-fed Americans I know.

So what is their secret? How is this possible? We would suggest that the reason has to do with relationships. Most of these people live in very tight-knit communities that go through everything together. There is a sense that "my people will be there for me" and that "I will never go through anything alone." There is also very real joy shared relationally with friends and family in these communities. In the end it is the relational joy that provides the foundation for life rather than the hardship.

GOOD NEWS! JOY CAN BE DEVELOPED

I (Chris) mentioned that when I first met my wife Jen she was a volunteer at the organization where I worked. I also mentioned that she struggled with depression and sometimes had trouble getting out of bed. Today, Jen and I teach people around the globe how to live with joy.

One of the reasons we are so confident of what is being taught in this book is because we have experienced joy for ourselves. We are now passing joy on to our sons, our family and friends, neighbors, strangers, and pretty much wherever we can. Joy changes everything!

As Jen and I developed exercises for the people at the center to practice, we practiced them as well. The interactive exercises had a profoundly transformational impact on both of us. We found that we smiled more often. We reflected on joy, talked about joyful memories, and shared joy stories with each other and those in our lives. Interactions became opportunities for the good stuff to spread. The information and exercises in this book have deeply changed our lives, transformed our parenting, invigorated our marriage, and changed how we approach life and relationships. We now run trainings, write blogs, develop resources, and speak on the power of joy!

In this book we want to help you learn the habits that transformed our lives and that brought so much hope and healing to people we have trained. We want to help you build your own joy house so that when it comes to joy, there is enough for you and some to share.

At the end of each habit chapter, we will have a joy workout to help you practice the skills that build the four habits of joy-filled people.

CHAPTER 2

The Brain Science of Joy

ON NOVEMBER 13, 2020 a special edition of *Time* magazine trumpeted the following headline, "The Power of Joy." The entire magazine was devoted to the topic. In 2015, Pixar and Disney released "Inside Out," an animated film that explored the brain and the central role of joy in our lives. The movie featured a group of adorable characters who represented the different emotions that often run the control center of our brains, and introduced us to the idea that we often feel the most like ourselves when Joy is in control. It also made the point that we can still be ourselves no matter which emotion is running the console of the brain. Harvard University has a webpage devoted to cultivating joy at work.[1] The Yale Center for Faith & Culture has launched a project titled "Theology of Joy & the Good Life."[2] It is hard to miss the fact that more and more people, and institutions, are beginning to emphasize the crucial role of joy in our lives.

The primary reason for this explosion of interest in joy is a technological breakthrough that makes it possible to scan brain activity in real time.[3] Before this, in order to study the brain you basically had to wait for someone to die and do an autopsy. It was not the most effective way to gather information about what was happening in the brain in real time as we engaged with life. This new ability to take pictures of the brain in action led to a surprising discovery that has revolutionized the priority we give to the importance of joy. One of the pioneers behind this revolution of joy was Dr. Allan Schore.[4] He has been called "the Einstein of psychoanalysis" and is recognized around the world for his work in combining the latest neuroscience with attachment theory and maturity development.[5] Dr. Schore was one of the first people to identify joy as the fuel on which the brain runs best.[6] The 1990s saw a number of key influencers spreading the importance of this revolution in neuroscience.[7] All of this activity led President George H. W. Bush to proclaim the 1990s "the decade of the brain."

WHAT IS JOY?

In his article "The Power of Joy," Jeffrey Kluger writes, "Defining joy is a fool's gambit—like trying to parse a joke or diagram love or lift a sand sculpture."[8] At some level, we would have to agree. Trying to define any experience will inevitably fall short, but it is also important to offer some type of definition that gives us a starting point for discussion. This is especially true in a book devoted to teaching people how to grow joy.

A few years ago, I (Chris) wrote a book with neuroscience specialist Dr. Jim Wilder, addiction recovery specialist Ed Khouri, and educator Sheila Sutton called *Joy Starts Here*. In our book we describe joy this way.

> Joy is the twinkle in someone's eyes, the smile from deep inside, the gladness that makes lovers run toward each other, the smile of a baby, the feeling of sheer delight that grows stronger as people who love each other lock eyes, what God feels when He makes His face shine over us, and the leap in our hearts when we hear the voice of someone we have been missing for a long time.[9]

Joy is a high-energy emotion related to knowing that someone is happy to see me. The relational happiness we feel when we experience spontaneous joy can also be experienced when we relive joyful moments from the past or anticipate joyful moments in the future. Perhaps you have had the common experience of feeling more joy looking forward to seeing someone than you actually felt once you were with them. The joy you felt while anticipating the connection was real, but the lack of joy at the actual encounter probably left you feeling sadness, shame, or anger. Anticipating joy in the future is a powerful motivator. People will go to great lengths to get to people with whom they expect to share joy. They will run through the proverbial brick wall for someone with whom they have a deep enough attachment. Just think of how many love songs, poems, and novels have been built around the theme of overcoming obstacles to be with the one who brings us joy.

Anticipating joy in the future is a powerful motivator.

Joy can also be found in our past and reexperienced. When we remember joyful events from the past and allow ourselves to relive them in our minds, we can actually experience the same feelings of joy all over again. As I sit here now and remember sharing the joy of hitting a game-winning home run, I can picture myself making eye contact with my wife and my kids in the crowd and how much fun it was to share that moment with them. It makes me smile even as I write this. If I actually sat down with my family and we relived that memory together, the joy would grow even more intense. Joy gets amplified as it is shared. The chances are high that once we shared the joy of that memory, we would launch into more stories of other times we shared joy together. Reliving joyful memories is a great way to spend a few minutes (or a few hours) and it always leaves us feeling greater peace—like I'm going to be okay.

From a neuroscience perspective, joy is always relational. This is because it is largely created by a right-hemisphere to right-hemisphere connection in the brain. When my right brain interacts with your right brain and we are happy to see each other (usually through eye contact), the result is joy.[10] There is a bonding or attachment element to the experience of joy that cannot be reproduced simply by medication, herbs, or drugs. Such feel-good chemicals as dopamine and endorphins are involved in the experience of shared joy,[11] but there is more to it than this.

HOW JOY WORKS—
UNDERSTANDING THE BIOLOGY OF JOY

Most of the problems we have in understanding joy come when we miss the important role relationships play in creating it. Not all *pleasure* is relational. But all *joy* is relational. Whether we feel that joy by remembering the past, anticipating the future, or experiencing the present, there is a relational component to joy, and it is that relational component that separates mere pleasure from real joy.

While joy can't be completely understood in terms of hormones and chemicals, it does help to understand something about them. There are four foundational chemicals/hormones that are often involved in our experience of sharing relational, glad-to-be-together joy with others.

Dopamine can be thought of as "the reward hormone." It gives a feeling of pleasure that we look forward to; hence, the idea of seeking a reward. Here is our attention chemical that tells us what to pay attention to. Dopamine is a neurotransmitter released in the brain stem that comes from experiences as diverse as playing with our kids, using drugs, jumping out of an airplane, or sexual stimulation. The problem with dopamine is that it is non-relational. It doesn't really care what creates the feeling of pleasure it craves. It doesn't care if I get sexual pleasure from my wife, from pornography, or from a prostitute. It is only interested in the "reward" we will feel when the pleasure comes. Many addictions revolve around creating a dopamine high, which gives us a temporary sense of pleasure, but it does not create a lasting sense of joy. Part of growing our maturity is learning to control our cravings for these highs by filling our lives with more relationally satisfying experiences.

Endorphins are natural pain relievers, the "feel-good" responses that are released through exercise and laughter. These are the chemicals that are responsible for what many call "a runner's high." When they are released, I feel alive and energetic like I am on a natural high. In this sense, they can be thought of as "happiness hormones." Infants get endorphins from noticing the joy on their mother's face, because she is glad to see them.[12] Over time, infants don't even need to know the person. They just need to be able to see the sparkle in their eyes that the person is happy to see them. Here is why we can sometimes make eye contact with a baby we don't know and share a smile that brings them real joy (and us too). We may never see them again, but in that moment, we shared some joy.

Oxytocin is commonly known as the "bonding hormone." Oxytocin receptors form the first few months after birth up to about three years of life because of warm, loving interaction.[13] It personalizes joy. Oxytocin works with other neurochemicals to help us better enjoy our interactions.[14] Whereas dopamine doesn't care how it finds pleasure, oxytocin is released because I am happy to be with you specifically. When I walk into a store and see someone I know shopping in the same store and we light up to see each other, that releases oxytocin. I'm thinking, "Hey, I know you!" That person may be someone I've only met once, or it may be an old friend I have known for years. Either way, it will create some level of joyful connection to see them.

Oxytocin is also the primary chemical being released when we fall in love. When I see my sweetheart and get a rush of joy and excitement, that is a very personalized bonding experience, not just the dopamine rush of seeing a pretty face. We feel loved and secure. This is a joy I only experience because of who I am with. When dopamine and oxytocin combine, we end up with the strong sense of reward to be with the one we love.

Serotonin helps us feel peaceful and quiet. It is known as an antidepressant. When released, it is like stepping on the brakes and slowing down the car. We can rest but still enjoy being connected. Serotonin is often paired with oxytocin so that being together doesn't have to require high-energy excitement or stimulation. We can enjoy being together while we take a breather and rest together. Serotonin is what helps us regulate our moods. When our brain learns to rest, we enjoy the on-demand release of serotonin as needed to help us calm down and feel refreshed. Serotonin helps us get more out of our dopamine and oxytocin responses by turning up the signals of these chemicals.[15]

From the perspective of one who is trying to build habits that lead to a joy-filled life, it is helpful to understand the difference between a dopamine or endorphin high and the bonded high produced by oxytocin. One is temporary and fleeting. The other creates attachment and builds relationships. It is also helpful to recognize our need for quiet and to understand that quiet doesn't always mean isolation. We can quiet ourselves relationally, and this practice will build a foundation for peace in our lives.

TWO ESSENTIAL BRAIN DEVELOPMENTS

Becoming a joy-filled person requires two primary developments in the brain. The first is the growth of a large joy center. The second is the construction of a pathway back to joy from each of the upsetting emotions we experience. We call these joy pathways.[16]

The joy center

Your joy center is located behind your right eye. Its technical name is the right orbital (as in the right eye) prefrontal (as in the front of your brain) cortex (the outermost layer of our brain where our highest-level brain function occurs). This part of your brain is largely undeveloped at birth, but it grows to become the captain of the emotional command center in the brain. This part of the brain remembers who we are, who our people are, how it is like us to act, and contains all sorts of information we need in order to bring the best version of ourselves into any situation we face. We call the right orbital prefrontal cortex "the joy center" partly because it is easier to say, but also because it grows with the experience of relational joy. The area of the brain that houses a well-developed joy center can expand to fill up nearly a third of the brain.[17] On the other hand, a poorly developed joy center can remain quite small and make it very difficult to live with joy, remain relational under stress, or act like ourselves when we get upset.

Joy pathways

The second area of brain development we need to experience if we are to become joy-filled people is the creation and strengthening of joy pathways. A joy pathway is a neurological path that helps us navigate from upsetting emotions in the back of our brain to the joy center in the front of our brain.[18]

As infants, we are not born with joy pathways in our brains. Because of this, we have no ability to act like ourselves when we get upset. One of the primary tasks of a parent when it comes to their child's emotional development is to recognize when they are experiencing an upsetting emotion and help them quiet from that emotion and return to joy. The more this happens, the more emotionally stable children become.

Infants and small children have to learn how to act like themselves despite the way they feel. This is not something that happens overnight. It also cannot happen without a lot of help. Such skills can only be developed relationally. We need to see others do it. We need them to help us do it. And we need it to happen with every difficult emotion we face—repeatedly.

As more mature people help babies and toddlers recover from their big emotions, a neurological pathway begins to develop in their brains. As this neural pathway develops it becomes stronger and more stable.[19] As it gets stronger it eventually wraps itself in white matter, which is the sign that a habit has formed.

White matter allows signals to be passed through the brain at super fast speeds. Most of the brain is composed of gray matter, which is not slow. It processes data at rates of about six cycles per second. But white matter can process data up to two hundred cycles per second. The result is that white matter allows us to develop instinctive reactions that are much faster than conscious thought. Once white matter develops around the pathways of the brain that allow us to return to joy, even young children can begin to remain relational, maintain a stable identity, and quiet themselves relatively quickly without even thinking about it. It can happen so fast that it seems to happen automatically. This is a sign that a well-formed joy pathway has been developed and has been wrapped in white matter.

"STUCK IN THE BACK OF MY BRAIN"

Most people have both underdeveloped joy centers and underdeveloped joy paths. As a result, I can find myself at age sixty still unable to cope with certain emotions because my brain never developed the neural pathways needed to recover from them. Instead, I get stuck in my upsetting emotions and live out of the fear centers in the back of my brain rather than living from the command center of joy in the front of the brain. All sorts of disorders, dysfunctions, addictions, and emotional problems arise from undeveloped joy pathways in the brain.[20]

To be clear—having a well-developed joy pathway doesn't mean you quickly stop feeling unpleasant emotions like fear, grief, anger, or despair and suddenly feel happiness instead. It means that these emotions don't trap you in the back of your brain without access to the command center. Well-developed joy pathways enable us to maintain a stable identity regardless of how we feel.[21] Without this I turn into a different person with every emotion I feel. That is how infants act. For example, have you ever heard someone say, "You won't like me when I'm mad"? They are essentially confessing that they have never built the maturity required to stay themselves when they get angry. Similarly, if people walk around us on eggshells because they never know when we are going to remain relational and act like ourselves and when we are going to turn into someone else by blowing up, melting down, or shutting down, it means we have never developed a strong pathway from those emotions back to the command center of the brain that remembers who we are and how it is like us to act.

When I (Marcus) first started learning about how the brain works and the importance of the joy center, joy pathways, and living from the front of my brain, I began to realize how much of my life was spent getting stuck in the back of my brain and trying to soothe myself and avoid further upset. It became obvious that I spent a lot of time and energy trying to avoid certain emotions because I didn't know how to deal with those emotions. This showed up first in my marriage. I began to notice that all it took was a certain tone of voice from my wife and I shut down relationally. I stopped acting like an adult and turned into a pouting little child. That wasn't a choice I was making. It was a well-developed habit that happened automatically. I had learned at a young age to shut up and disappear when someone wasn't happy to be with me. Here I was at age fifty, still following the same patterns.

Understanding brain science made me realize for the first time that the problem wasn't my wife. The problem was that my brain had gone into a cramp and I had lost access to my higher-level brain functions. In a sense, I was trapped living with only half of my brain engaged. As you can imagine, there are far different strategies involved in recovery if you think your wife is the problem than there will be if you think having half your brain offline is the problem. When I thought she was the problem, I would spend hours rehearsing reasons as to why I was justified in how I was acting. When I began to treat my shut-down brain as the problem, it led me in a completely different direction for solutions.

Again, let me be clear. I am not saying that my wife never did anything wrong and was never at fault in her actions. I am saying that we handled the situation much differently when I was acting like myself and remaining relational than when I was shut down and pouting.

An example like this can help us understand the relationship between joy and maturity. Since the joy center is also the command center of the brain, I only remain relational and act like myself when I am living with this part of my brain engaged. My ability to recover from difficult emotions and still keep the command center in charge is what marks me as a mature person. The more easily overwhelmed I am emotionally, the less mature I will be. The more weight it takes to make the system shut down, the more mature I will be.

SHRINKING THE JOY GAP

All of us live with a "joy gap" in our lives. As Chris and I say in our book *The 4 Habits of Joy-Filled Marriages*,[22] a joy gap is the amount of time between moments of joy. If we know that several times each day we are going to experience five or ten minutes of relational joy and that we are going to have a break at some point, our capacity to handle the hard stuff in life gets bigger. But when we don't know if we are going to get a chance to rest or a chance to spend time with someone who is happy to see us, our emotions can start to go downhill quickly. Life can begin spiraling into depression when sharing joy with others begins to feel hopeless.

Many of us may not have thought about our emotional challenges as joy gaps, but joy—and the confidence that there is joy to come—play a tremendous role in giving us

the capacity to deal with the hardships of life. What neuroscience has
been teaching us is that creating joy
is a more predictable event than we
may have thought. Instead of waiting
and hoping that we will get zapped
with joy from out of the blue, there
are concrete habits we can develop
that make joy a much more predictable part of life. We refer to the
process of developing those habits as
"building a joy house."

What neuroscience has been teaching us is that creating joy is a more predictable event than we may have thought.

BUILDING A JOY HOUSE

As we saw in the last chapter, building a joy house starts
with laying the foundation. This foundation focuses on
calming and appreciating as the skills needed to grow the
joy center of the brain. This requires a regular routine of
joy workouts. To help you get started, we have included
several of these workouts in the book.

The joy center. We lay the foundation of our joy house by growing a large joy center in our brains. The two key habits we need to grow that center are calming and appreciating.

- Calming
- Appreciating

Joy pathways. We develop the framework of our joy house by developing joy pathways from the back of the brain to the front where our joy center is located. The two habits most needed in order to strengthen these pathways are storytelling and attacking toxic thoughts.

- Storytelling
- Attacking Toxic Thoughts

Once the house is built, our goal is to fill it with a lifetime of satisfying habits rather than merely pleasurable distractions.

As we move to the next chapter, it is time to start unpacking these four habits and introduce the Joy Workouts that can help you begin to build your own joy house. Like any construction project, building your joy house will take some work. But in the end, it is definitely worth it.

CHAPTER 3

Calming: Habit #1

PANIC ATTACKS ARE THE WORST. I (Marcus) had only ever experienced one on a few occasions. All of a sudden, while at the Denver airport, I found myself telling my wife that I needed to sit down. I thought it might be altitude sickness, but soon realized it was more than that. It didn't stop. I could feel the high energy of anxiety begin to course through my body and just keep growing as we made our way to the hotel. I couldn't sleep that night. The next morning it came back. My face was hot, my right hand was shaking, and the very fact that I didn't know how to make it stop made it worse. Sometimes it came like a stabbing pain in my heart, sometimes like a punch in the gut, sometimes it just snuck up on me, usually starting in my face or my hands.

At first my anxiety was about money. I was completely upside down financially and it looked like I might be missing my next paycheck or two. But it felt like something broke. Before I knew it, the feeling of anxiety had moved into my body like an unwanted companion. If I had an hour out of my day without anxiety in my body, it just became a reason to fear how soon it would come back. My world felt booby-trapped. There was literally nothing I could do that didn't risk triggering a spike in anxiety. This went on for over a year. It was awful!

Because of this intense battle, I became highly motivated to learn about ways to increase my emotional capacity. Like Chris, I had a relationship with Dr. Jim Wilder and asked him for help a few times. He and I wrote the book *Rare Leadership* together around that time, and he was very generous in helping me understand what was happening and how to carve out a path forward. I called Chris (my coauthor on this book) several times. On more than one occasion, when I needed some help snapping out of a spiral, Chris was there to offer a listening ear and some wise counsel. I went to several counselors and talked to a lot of people looking for help. Unexpectedly, I also found that I developed a great deal more compassion for people who struggled with emotions they didn't know how to handle.

Gradually, I began to have a few hours a day without my old "friend." Then, one day in the spring, I realized I'd gone a whole day without feeling its grip in my body. It felt good to be able to breathe. I was beginning to realize that feeling anxiety wasn't going to be a permanent condition. That realization by itself was a great relief.

THE FOUR HABITS

My battle with anxiety taught me the importance of calming. It also led me to learn a lot of tools and tips for quieting my body when it felt out of control. The four habits taught in this book became my lifelines to being functional. I needed to tear down the fear house I had built inside and use the CASA habits to start building a joy house.

Calming

I learned that calming isn't simply a choice. It does no good to tell someone to "just calm down." I also learned that sometimes I can quiet myself and sometimes I need help. There are strategies for calming yourself when you are alone, but there are also times when having other people around makes a world of difference. Before my battle, I had not realized just how physical emotions could be. It helped me understand that much of what we mean when we say we need to calm ourselves is that we need to quiet our bodies. Our body is the canvas for the brain, so noticing and quieting our body helps us reduce tension everywhere.

Appreciating

While I was in a state of anxiety, it was almost impossible to practice appreciation. I could be grateful and say thank you, but this is not the same thing. For example, one morning I poured myself a cup of coffee in one of my favorite mugs. I let myself feel the cool of the mug and smell the aroma of the coffee as I was intentionally trying to appreciate the experience. The problem was that I could only stay in that state of appreciation for about two seconds. I held the cool mug with the nice aroma up to my nose, took a deep breath and thought to myself, "This is the stupidest thing I have ever done."

The reality is that appreciation doesn't fix our problems and it is not a magic bullet that suddenly makes us feel better. Compared to the magnitude of the concerns that weighed me down, a cup of coffee felt pretty meaningless. In some ways, however, that is the point. Appreciation is about giving yourself permission to enjoy the little things in life in the midst of all the junk. Appreciation redirects your attention to savor the good stuff instead of ruminating on the bad. According to Dr. Wilder, being able to enter a state of appreciation for five consecutive minutes two to three times a day for thirty days can change the chemistry in your brain so joy becomes your new normal instead of fear. Practicing appreciation also helps you grow your joy center and strengthen joy pathways.

Storytelling

While I was in the midst of my struggle, I began to notice that when I told stories about my emotions, those stories ended in defeat. I simply told people how bad my struggles were. There was no hope in the stories. One of the strategies Chris helped me understand was that I needed to tell stories of times when I returned to joy, handled the emotion well, or when I felt the emotion but still handled myself like an adult. Those stories served as reminders that I was not defined by failure or doomed to defeat. The more stories I collected, the more the library in my brain started to fill its shelves with tales of success. This increased my confidence and helped my brain learn that my upsetting emotions were not the end of the world. Collecting stories about feeling hard emotions and handling life well anyway, or bouncing back quickly, helps us correct the mental narratives that can undo us emotionally. Good, brain-friendly stories can create new pathways in the brain to help us stay relational and return to joy faster from our upsetting emotions.

Attacking toxic thinking

One of the things I learned about anxiety specifically is that anxiety is always rooted in our imagination. Whereas fear is a reaction to danger or potential pain (like the reaction to unexpectedly seeing a spider in the bathroom sink), anxiety can jump from imagination to catastrophic nightmare in a heartbeat. Anxiety creates a feeling of fear just by anticipating that there might be a spider in the sink. Overcoming the negative control of most emotions requires getting control of our thought life.

Anxiety can jump from imagination to catastrophic nightmare in a heartbeat.

Each of these four habits represents a group of activities that can be done on our own or with others. Practicing them with other people is an essential part of turning these activities into habits. In this chapter, we want to introduce you to four specific practices that help build the habit of calming ourselves from upset emotions and quieting our bodies.

BEST PRACTICES FOR CALMING

In the next few pages, we want to introduce you to the four best practices we have found for quieting your body and calming your emotions. Right up front, we want to say that calming or quieting doesn't mean making an emotion disappear. It means reducing it to the point that it is manageable.

These four practices can be remembered with the word BEST—as in, this is a list of BEST practices for calming emotions.

Breathe in a box

This practice, also called "four-square" or "resetting your breath" breathing, is a common strategy taught in the military for dealing with pressure situations. One of the first physical reactions we have to overwhelming emotions is that our breathing becomes shallow. We may even hold our breath when we become stressed, anxious, or upset.

Taking deep breaths helps us regain control of our bodies and helps to quiet our emotions. Deep breathing activates the brakes of our nervous system so we can shift out of high-energy fear responses to low-energy rest states. For box breathing, we simply empty our lungs, inhale through our nose to the count of four, hold our breath to a count of four, then exhale to the count of four and hold to the count of four. We can do this several times and increase or decrease the count as needed. You might try breathing in a box two or three times right now and see how it makes you feel.

Exaggerate the emotion

As we have already mentioned, calming isn't simply a choice. There is a process needed in order to practice and learn this skill. Part of that process is to exaggerate the emotion and then quiet it, much like removing tension from muscles by bracing then relaxing. When we say to exaggerate the emotion, we are specifically referring to the physical reaction that emotion creates. Here are a few examples.

Fear—When babies under two months old feel fear they have an involuntary reaction in which they gasp and throw their hands over their heads. This is sometimes called the Moro reflex or the startle reflex. Building on this instinctive response to fear, Dr. Wilder and Ed Khouri developed an exercise called "Shalom your body."[1] It works like this. Find a private place to go (this might look strange in public). Throw your hands over your head and gasp as you quickly breathe in. Then, slowly breathe out as you lower your arms and clasp your hands at your chest or waist. You can do this three or four times. The exercise is designed to calm your fear response, which will help you get control over the anxious feelings in your body. It won't likely get rid of all your fear, but should make the feelings more manageable.

Anger—Most of us are familiar with "the Hulk pose" made famous by the "rock star" of the Avengers movies, when he would clench his fists in front of his body, and flex his biceps, while scowling and grunting in anger. The Hebrew word for anger is actually the same word used for "nose," which is a good reminder that people often flare their nostrils when they get angry. A good way to exaggerate the feeling of anger is to find a private place, do the "Hulk pose" and flare your nostrils. It can also help to wring a towel or something like that. The goal is to get the energy of the emotion to peak so that it can begin to quiet. After increasing the energy in this way, take several deep breaths and refocus on the task at hand.

Shame—The feeling of shame triggers the vagus nerve network in the back of our neck so that we instinctively drop our heads. This is why encouraging someone can sometimes be referred to as "lifting their head." It is a sign that you are not ashamed of them and want to help them feel like themselves again. When we feel shame, we can follow a similar process to the one described above. Go somewhere private. Hang your head and feel the shame. Then lift your head and inhale deeply. Repeat this process a few times.

Soothe your senses

This practice is about doing something to change your environment or your body chemistry. Sometimes it helps to shock your system like taking a cold shower or splashing cold water on your face. Other times, we need to comfort ourselves by snuggling in a chair with a weighted blanket or taking a hot bath. The idea is to do something physical to get control of your body's response to your emotions. Here are a few other options:

- Rub your arms from top to bottom as if you are wiping the tension out of them.
- Use your right hand to rub your left shoulder, and your left hand to rub your right shoulder.
- Move your eyes from side to side while keeping your head perfectly still. Look up. Look down. Look side to side. This helps distract your brain from your upsetting thoughts.

It is probably worth noting that many addictions start by trying to find ways to soothe our upset emotions and relieve tension from our bodies. We drink alcohol, watch porn, take drugs, and eat way too much ice cream in an attempt to soothe our bodies from the upset emotions we feel. Of course, there are many unwanted side effects to such addictions, which is why learning these BEST practices is an important part of addiction recovery as well as managing our everyday emotions.

Tell yourself the truth

Negative emotions are not our enemies. They serve an important purpose. They serve as an alarm to alert us that something needs our attention. Our problems arise when they are triggered by false beliefs or when we cannot quiet them. Our brain has two engines for our emotions: our thought life and our reactions to the environment. Telling yourself the truth focuses on the cognitive engine on the left side of the brain that ties a narrative to our negative emotions. We will have a lot more to say about telling yourself the truth when we come to the fourth habit of joy-filled people—attacking toxic thinking. For now, it is helpful to understand that part of calming ourselves from upsetting emotions involves dealing with some of the destructive thoughts that often accompany our troubling emotions.

It is important to know that it is very difficult to "think your way" out of any emotion. Generally, we just dig ourselves into a deeper pit because our minds get stuck in the fact that we are in such a big battle. It can also be helpful to realize that it is okay to distract ourselves from negative thoughts. We don't always have to "defeat" them or play tug-of-war with them. Sometimes just distracting ourselves and shifting our attention from the battle so that we think about something else is enough to break the tension and stop the downward spiral. For long-term success, however, we are going to need to learn how to reprogram the faulty thinking patterns that accompany our troubling emotions. Our chapter on attacking toxic thinking will focus on how to do that.

Here is a simple thought strategy that can help you tell yourself the truth as you quiet upsetting emotions. We call it VCR—Validate, Comfort, Recover.

Validate—tell yourself the truth about how you are feeling. Give it a name. Identify how big it is.

"I am angry. I am really angry. I feel like breaking things. If I had a bazooka I'd probably shoot something right now."

"I am scared. I am only sort of scared, though. This just startled me."

"I feel disgusted with that person. I wish they would just get out of here. On a scale of one to ten, my disgust is probably at level six."

Comfort—tell yourself the truth about how to handle your emotion and ask, "What do I need when I feel this way?"

"I am too angry to talk about this right now. I should probably leave or at least stay quiet."

"I was startled, but I'll be okay. I can take a deep breath and keep going."

"My disgust is not so great that I cannot treat this person with kindness. It would be like me to do something good for them."

Recover—This is not so much a step in the process as a sign that the process has worked. I no longer feel overwhelmed but can remain relational and act like myself despite how I feel.

HAVE A PLAN

A second strategy that can help with the battle for the mind is making a simple one- or two-step plan for what you are going to do next. A few years ago I (Marcus) wrote a book with Stefanie Hinman called *Building Bounce: How to Grow Emotional Resilience*.[2] Stefanie is a mother and an art therapist who specializes in helping people recover from childhood trauma. As we were working on the book, Stefanie made a statement that has resonated with me ever since. She said that among mental health professionals, hope is defined as having a plan. I had never thought about it that simply before. It made a lot of sense. Depression comes when I have no hope, because there is no plan that can fix my problem. Anxiety comes when I fear the trouble I will have to face, because I either have no plan or have no faith in my plan for the future. An important part of telling yourself the truth is creating a simple plan that gives some hope. Tell yourself the truth that the plan may not fix everything—but it will take you in a positive direction.

Calming strategies like these BEST practices can be very helpful with mild to moderate emotions. When we have really big emotions, we may need to practice "extreme quieting" that takes things to a whole new level.

Extreme quieting may involve doing jumping jacks or something physical to burn off the excess adrenaline coursing through our bodies. It can take twenty to thirty minutes for the adrenaline triggered by panic to subside. One plan I sometimes followed when dealing with a panic attack involved running in place, holding my head still and moving my eyes up and down then left and right, singing happy birthday to myself (which often made me laugh), and breathing deeply while rubbing the tension out of my arms. I sometimes did this for up to ten or fifteen minutes as I burned off the extra energy in my body and began to quiet. Extreme quieting is just a way of saying I need an extended time to quiet.

INTERACTIVE QUIETING

Interactive quieting refers to activities we do with others that help us to calm our strong emotions and quiet our bodies. When my (Chris) son was a toddler, the sound of the coffee grinder frightened him.[3] With a panicked expression on his face, he would cry anytime he heard the sound of grinding coffee beans.

One day, I was making my morning coffee and I used the grinder. A screech came from the next room as my son heard the sound of the grinder. I peeked around the corner to watch as he darted behind the couch for cover. This was intense for him!

Jen knelt to his level, then sat near him. He carefully watched Jen's face in order to gauge whether he was going to survive this terrible encounter. While tracking Jen's face, he watched as she used her face and voice to validate and comfort him. "This is scary!" she said while nestled next to him. "You don't like this sound!" After matching his fear with her facial expressions and voice tone, she then shifted into compassion while speaking in a comforting tone. I watched as her bottom lip jutted out and she asked, "Do you want Mommy's arms?" and wrapped him up.

He moved to her lap and set his sights on watching me with the grinder. He turned to Jen's face and after a few rounds of watching Jen's face and listening to her words and soothing tones, he settled in and appeared more peaceful. Jen rubbed his back while speaking softly into his ear. The intense fear calmed down. He shifted to curiosity. He then roamed around the room a bit while keeping a close eye on the coffee grinder in the kitchen. His face softened and his voice normalized. He wanted to investigate the grinder, which was now in his mother's hands. After checking it out, he pushed the button on the scary grinder. Soon, he decided the grinder was not so threatening after all. Now it was a fun toy to play with!

Had Jen dismissed our son's fears, ignored his cries, or even gotten angry, this would have turned out differently. He could have learned a very unhelpful lesson about big feelings. He could have felt all alone. He may have learned emotions were something to be feared and avoided at all costs! Thankfully, Jen came to the rescue by kneeling to his level, joining his distress, matching his energy levels, attuning with him then showing him how to calm down. The process of using her face and voice (words) to practice the VCR process worked so our son could feel his emotions in the presence of safe people and calm down enough to feel more manageable.

Interactive quieting refers to the relational dance that happens when we encounter high-energy emotions. We mirror what people are feeling, then we slowly calm down enough to make the feelings more manageable while we stay connected. It took several rounds for Jen and our boy to reach his relational footing, but he arrived at the safety of the harbor after enduring the storm of his fearful feelings. Had Jen gotten stuck herself, defensive or even non-relational in that moment, he would have felt alone, afraid, and overwhelmed.[4] Sadly, if this had happened, it could have been fodder for avoidance behavior, including lies and distorted beliefs, to arise from this kind of painful experience.

We use interactive quieting to stay connected in high-energy emotions so the interaction can continue without "going over the top" and turning violent and aggressive or provoking some other unwanted reaction.

NURTURE A RHYTHM

The BEST practices we have discussed are ways of calming our body and our brains when they are upset. However, an important element of building the habit of calming is the practice of nurturing a rhythm. We all need times of high-energy joy and low-energy rest. Nurturing a rhythm means protecting ourselves from always having to be "on." We can't always be in a high energy state. Sometimes we need alone time without a lot of noise or emotional demands. And sometimes we need quiet time with just one or two other people where we can enjoy being together in a low-energy state.

Let's say you just finished a basketball game and you are sweaty and tired. Or maybe you had a long day at the office. You don't want to do anything high energy, but you don't really want to be alone either. The idea of spending some "downtime" with a few friends might be just what you need. I (Chris) once spent a whole day teaching and was looking forward to a quiet dinner with friends at the end of the day, but our evening together turned into another high-energy event that demanded more of my capacity and focus than I had available. Experiences like this have taught me to guard my energy levels and make sure I speak up about my needs.

We all need a manageable rhythm in which we balance times of high-energy joy with low-energy peace. Some of this starts with just paying attention to our calendar. We need to plan ahead for the rest we need. It is also important to pay attention to our own sense of being overwhelmed and recognizing when we need a break. Taking a breather can keep us from doing things we regret. For example, the other night I (Marcus) was out for a nice walk with my wife. We were talking about projects we wanted to do around the house. My wife was getting excited and feeling a lot of energy about the subject, but it was starting to overwhelm me. If I had noticed the warning signs, I could have asked for a break before coming back to the subject later. Instead, I ignored the warning signs and ended up shutting down and unable to share her joy. As a result, I hurt her feelings and pulled the plug on our happy evening together. It could have been avoided by paying attention to the signals of emotional overwhelm and suggesting a break. This is all part of recognizing our need for rhythm.

LAYING THE FOUNDATION FOR OUR JOY HOUSE

Since my unexpected battle with anxiety, I (Marcus) have worked very hard to build my joy house by laying a foundation of calming and appreciation, telling joy stories, and attacking toxic thoughts quickly. (We will address these next three habits in the upcoming chapters.) I am not anxiety-free. I can still get triggered. But it doesn't happen very often, and my capacity to bounce back has grown. It has been a long time since anxiety has felt like an inevitable companion.

As you seek to lay the foundation for your joy house, we encourage you to be intentional about using these BEST practices for calming on a daily basis and nurturing a sustainable rhythm for life. If you are not in a major battle with your emotions currently that is good. It is easiest to build these skills while dealing with mild or moderate emotions. If you are smack-dab in the middle of an emotional crisis, you may not notice any immediate relief by practicing these skills, because it can take a couple of months before we notice how much has changed. Even so, there is no time like the present to get started.

JOY WORKOUTS FOR CALMING

Learning to calm our emotions and rest, like any habit, requires intentionality and practice. When we can rest on the good days, the habit is more likely to be there on the bad days when fatigue, upsetting emotions, and difficulties run rampant.

With practice, we can notice what calming does to our mind and body. Noticing what happens when we rest and calm down helps our brain pay attention to the changes that come with the soothing effects powering down our mind and body. Observing these changes is an essential part of forming new habits, because we start to notice when we need a breather.

JOY WORKOUT #1—*Box breathing*

1. Find a comfortable place to practice box breathing. You first empty your lungs to the count of four, then take a deep breath in while you count to four. Next, hold your breath to the count of four, then exhale

to the count of four. We recommend you try several several rounds of this to feel calmer and more relaxed.

2. Scan your body from the top of your head to the bottom of your feet to notice what this breathing exercise feels like. Notice your breathing, muscle tension, and thoughts. Did anything change?

3. Now try box breathing again, only this time around reflect on something you feel thankful for today while you complete Steps 1 and 2. Notice if gratitude makes a difference in your experience.

4. Now try the exercise with a friend or family member and discuss the experience.

JOY WORKOUT #2—*Exaggerating emotions*

The goal with the calming practices is to establish "muscle memory" for our mind and body to grow accustomed to the quieting steps. As we try these sequences during the calm moments of life, they will feel more natural during stormy seasons. If we do not practice in the calm times it will be harder to utilize when we are upset and overwhelmed. Go on, have some fun and exaggerate your emotions and see what you notice!

1. Find a comfortable position to practice exaggerating the emotion for fear. Refer to the instructions in this chapter or visit YouTube to watch the *Shalom*

my body example for the startle (Moro) reflex.[5] Try several rounds of this exercise.

2. When you finish, scan your body to see what changes after doing the first step.

3. Even though you may not be mad at this moment, let's have a bit of fun exaggerating the emotion for anger. Even though it may feel strange trying this step, try the best you can.

4. Now exaggerate the emotion for shame, even though you may not be feeling ashamed right now. Simply lower your head for a moment while you take a deep breath in; then look up and breathe for several deep breaths. When you look up, make a positive statement about something you enjoy about yourself. Try several rounds and come up with a new positive statement about yourself each time. (For example, I may say the following words when I look up: "I like that I am a caring person who loves well.")

5. When you finish, scan your body to see what changes after doing the step.

6. Now try the exercise with a friend or family member and discuss the experience.

JOY WORKOUT #3—*Soothing my senses*

The brain has a novelty detector that says, "Pay attention!" when we try something new. Thanks to dopamine, our brain responds positively when we try to create new habits that will eventually be woven into the fabric of our character. With practice, these habits become familiar and turn into reflexes we will use without having to think about it. Now, we practice soothing our senses to see what we notice.

1. Find a comfortable position to practice soothing your senses. Try the following sequence, then pay attention to what you notice after doing the exercises.

2. Rub your arms from the top of your shoulder all the way down to the tips of your fingers. Use your right hand on your left arm, and your left hand on your right arm. Try to picture yourself using your hands to iron out wrinkles from a T-shirt as you move your hand down your arm. Inhale deeply when you start with your shoulder, then exhale as you move down the arm. Squeeze your fingers as you finish and try this several times.

3. Pause to scan your body to see what you notice.

4. Next, rub your left shoulder with your right hand, and your right shoulder with your left hand as you breathe deeply. Do this several times.

5. Pause to scan your body to see what you notice.

6. While you continue the deep breathing, move your eyes from side to side and up and down while you keep your head still. Now continue the deep breathing while you stretch your arms up to the ceiling,

using your left hand to pull your right hand straight up, and vice versa.

7. Pause to scan your body to see what you notice.
8. Now try the exercise with a friend or family member and discuss the experience.

JOY WORKOUT #4—*Telling yourself the truth*

The VCR process is an excellent resource for navigating unpleasant emotions and learning to stay connected during big feelings. In this exercise, we focus on identifying qualities about ourselves that tend to get lost when we are upset.

1. Find a comfortable seat and use your journal or phone to write down your thoughts to the following questions. If you prefer, you can simply reflect on each step.
2. Write out or verbalize what validation sounds like for feeling sad about something in your life.

   • Validation is when we tell the truth about what we feel, and say what we see and hear. We may say something like, "I feel sad today about being on this diet where I can't eat sugar. I really miss my ice cream!"

3. Next, write out or verbalize what you would say to comfort yourself.

- Comfort is when we tell the truth about how we can handle our emotions and we discover what we need right now. We may come up with something we can still be thankful for even while we feel our feelings. This could be "I am glad that even though I must avoid ice cream, I can spend time with my family this evening, which will be meaningful. This time will help me feel better."

4. Finish by stating a simple plan for what you could do next while you feel your sad feelings.

   - An example would be, "Because I'm sad I cannot have ice cream right now, and I'm glad to be with my family this evening, I will reflect on what I'm thankful for to see if this lifts my mood. If feeling grateful doesn't help, I may take a short walk around the block for some fresh air . . ."

5. What can you predict will get lost in the flurry of upset feelings when you feel mad, sad, afraid, ashamed, hopeless, and disgusted? Another way to look at this question is to think about what you value when you feel happy that gets lost when you are upset.

   - What happens in you when you are upset? This includes your thoughts, beliefs, feelings, cravings, body, and behaviors.

- What tends to get lost in how you view yourself during these upsetting moments?

6. Does it feel natural and easy to validate yourself when you are upset, or do you become critical or harsh to yourself? Write out a few common examples that come to mind for what you say to yourself when you are upset; this may be positive or negative.

7. When you are with someone who is upset, is it easy to validate them? Why or why not? What conditions make it easy or difficult to validate people in their distress?

8. Find a friend or family member to share your thoughts and discuss these topics together.

CHAPTER 4

Appreciating: Habit #2

SEVERAL YEARS AGO, I (Marcus) was invited to do some training for a group of people who had been overseas. They had devoted their lives to helping the poor, providing education for children, and offering spiritual direction for the adults in various parts of Africa. The task often meant living in rural locations that lacked many of the comforts we take for granted in the United States. Sometimes it was hard not to become frustrated with all the challenges that had to be overcome. Equipment often broke down. People could be undependable. The other workers often seemed to create more problems than they solved. One lady in particular had developed a highly critical attitude about just about everything. She didn't like the food, the heat, the hassles, and, at some level, she didn't even like the people. This went on long enough that her supervisor called her into a meeting to let her know that if her attitude didn't change, she was going to be sent home.

The story shocked me. It wasn't shocking that a frustrating situation could spark a critical attitude. Most of us know what that is like. It was shocking because the woman telling me the story was one of the most joy-filled people I had ever met. To learn that she had not always been this way intrigued me.

When she smiled at me, I could almost tell she wanted me to ask how she turned things around. So I did. "What is your secret?" I asked. "How did you go from being someone who nearly got fired for having such a negative attitude to becoming one of the most joyful people in the organization?"

She looked at me with a twinkle in her eye and said, "Gratitude." She explained that the confrontation with her supervisor got her attention. She realized she needed to change, so she decided to do the opposite of complaining. She decided to become the most grateful person in the group. From that day on she began keeping a journal that focused entirely on what there was to appreciate about her situation. She found something to like about everyone she met and about every event in her day. In just a few days, she saw a difference. In a few weeks, she was a noticeably different person. By the time I met her, she had been practicing a lifestyle of appreciation and gratitude for nearly twenty years—and it showed.

One of the observations Chris and I have made through the years is that no matter how bad life gets, there is always something to appreciate. One of the scenes that drove this home for me came from the movie *The Last Samurai*. In this scene, Katsumoto, the leader of a samurai village, is dealing with the possible end of life as he knows it. The government and the culture are changing. They are becoming more Western in their dress, in the way they conduct business, and in the way they wage war. For hundreds of years, the samurai were the ultimate warriors. Their counsel was sought. They were respected. But that was all changing. In fact, they were becoming an obstacle to the forces of change.

Katsumoto was pondering a war he knew would cost him his life and likely signal the end of the samurai way of life. The weight of the world seemed to be hanging on his shoulders, yet in the midst of all this he took time to stroll through a grove of cherry trees so he could enjoy their beauty. He didn't just notice the beauty. He studied it. He spent time enjoying the experience. In the midst of all of his problems, he was taking time to quiet himself and appreciate beauty. It was a wonderful picture of someone going back to the foundation

Appreciation may be the single most common habit of joy-filled people.

of calming and appreciating to help restore the resilience that would be needed for the hard things to come.

Appreciation may be the single most common habit of joy-filled people. It is also the practice that will most quickly grow your capacity for joy. If you want to build a big joy center in the front of your brain and lay a solid foundation for your joy house, appreciation is the fastest way to do it.

FEAR VS. JOY

Our brains are natural amplifiers. They are good at taking low-level sounds and making them bigger. Sometimes the brain amplifies joy, and sometimes it amplifies fear. If we are not intentional about training our brain to bring joy into focus, it will always default to focusing on fear.

Appreciation trains the attention system in our brains to scan for the good stuff in life and pay attention to joyful things. Fear trains our brain to focus on ways to minimize the danger in our lives. It abandons joy and amplifies damage control. Over time—often without realizing it—our brains learn whether joy or fear is more important to us. If it realizes that we are more concerned with what there is to fear, it amplifies all of the fears and potential fears in our environment. If it learns that we value joy, it begins to amplify what there is in life to appreciate.

If our brains learn to focus on fear, we get good at fear-mapping our world. This means that wherever we go, we notice potential danger and focus on that. Consider the case of the woman whose fear-mapping landed her in bed with a stranger she didn't even find attractive. The process started when she was at a bar with some friends. A rough-looking biker walked in and her fear-bonded brain immediately lit up and paid attention to this new development. She kept glancing over at the stranger as her brain amplified the potential threat.

The biker noticed her looking his way a few times and misread the signal. He got up from his stool and walked over to her table to talk to her. In her mind the alarms were going off, but not in a good way. Her brain decided the best way to minimize damage in this situation was to be nice to the guy. She was too scared to tell him to leave, so she made small talk and the next thing she knew, he pulled up a chair and offered to buy her a drink. She was too afraid to decline the drink, and out of fear continued to practice damage control by trying to be friendly.

You can probably see where this is going. Soon he offered her a ride on his bike. Out of fear she said yes, and even though it was the last thing she wanted, by the end of the evening they ended up at a hotel having sex. The story reminds us how often we create problems for ourselves when we live out of fear rather than joy.

One of the reasons we focus on appreciation is that it trains our brains to run on the fuel of joy rather than fear. Left untrained, our brains will naturally run on fear.

Just imagine planting a garden, then disregarding it. If we simply let it grow without any follow-up care, what will happen to this patch of land? The weeds will quickly take over and pull resources from the plants we want to see flourish. This is what can happen with the brain's attention system. Without training it to run on the fuel of joy, our brain will focus on fears. The weeds of fear will dominate our thoughts and feelings and sap all our strength and energy. Let's look at these opposing fuels.

THE FEAR-FUELED BRAIN

The fear-fueled brain looks for what needs to be avoided rather than embraced. For those of us who live this way, we can find that we spend far too much time and expend far too much emotional energy avoiding difficult emotions. With every emotion we have to avoid, our world gets smaller. If I can't handle anger and have to avoid getting angry or dealing with angry people, my world shrinks a little bit. If I can't handle fear and have to avoid anything that triggers anxiety, my world shrinks even more. You get the idea. In some ways, the only thing our brains really fear is an emotion we can't handle.

Living with a fear-fueled brain is like building a fear house in our inner world rather than a joy house. It is a miserable thing to live with a fear house inside.

Here are some characteristics of a fear-fueled brain or an internal world built on a foundation of fear.

- We scan for threats rather than good things to enjoy.
- We feel guarded and avoid vulnerability. Self-preservation is key!
- We often give fear-based guidance rather than desire-driven wisdom. One avoids pain while the other focuses on how to stay our relational selves.
- We expect worst-case scenarios and often can't even imagine a best-case scenario.
- We are driven by self-preservation. Thus, fear dominates our time and energy rather than joy.

Routinely reflecting or ruminating on the things that bother, frighten, hurt, and annoy us trains our brain's attention system to scan for threats. Learning to practice appreciation and reflecting on joy from our past trains our brain to expect joy in the future. The brain that is trained to run on joy will scan the environment for good things to enjoy. We look for the beautiful aspects of life rather than scan for what can cause us pain.

The right hemisphere, the emotional engine, tells the left hemisphere, the cognitive engine, what to focus on. The right hemisphere needs to be trained if we are going to focus on what is there to appreciate and enjoy. Without this practice in place, the left brain will naturally focus on problems that need to be solved.

THE JOY-FUELED BRAIN

Joy is a relational experience. It comes from knowing you are the reason for the twinkle in someone's eye or the smile on their face. This doesn't mean you have to be with someone else to feel joy. You can feel joy remembering how it felt or you can feel joy anticipating what is to come. If you have ever had a group of really good friends, you can often feel joy by retelling the stories of your experiences together. As I write this I am thinking about a day at the lake with some of my friends. It was a June day, we had gone swimming and diving, and were sitting on a blanket playing cards. I remember feeling like it was the perfect day. Sometimes remembering one story like that kindles another memory and then another one and before you know it, you have spent five to ten minutes living in a state of joy.

When your brain learns that you like to do this regularly, it begins to amplify memories, experiences, and opportunities for experiencing this kind of joy. On the other hand, if our brains learn that we crave non-relational addictions, it can amplify those just as easily. This is one of the reasons that learning to reprogram our brains to amplify joy is an important part of overcoming addiction.

The reason joy and fear are so foundational to the way we live is that they control the relational circuitry in our brains. There is a social system in every brain that controls whether we feel like ourselves or not. This system is run by our RCs—relational circuits. When our RCs are firing on all cylinders, our relational self becomes present and we tend to feel and act like ourselves. But when these RCs start to misfire or shut down altogether our non-relational self comes out. When this happens we live out of fear rather than joy. We become problem-focused, anxiety-prone, non-relational, and motivated by damage control.

I (Chris) recently wrote a book called *The Joy Switch*. The core idea in this book is that we all have a joy switch in our brains that controls whether our RCs stay on or start to dim. When my switch is on, it is easy to act like myself, remain relational, and regulate my emotions. However, when the switch starts to dim or goes off altogether, I lose access to the part of my brain that remembers who I am and how it is like me to act.

Have you ever had the experience of feeling sad or

stuck in some upsetting emotion when a friend sat down next to you? If you feel joy that your friend is present, it can flip your joy switch on. This doesn't mean that all of your sadness goes away, but in the midst of your sadness, there is now relational joy as well. That joy gives you the emotional capacity you need to handle your sadness without getting overwhelmed. Having your friend there, helps your relational brain stay engaged so that you feel more like yourself in spite of your sadness.

Joy-fueled brains are not brains that never feel upsetting emotions. They are brains that operate with the joy switch on most of the time and learn how to flip the joy switch back on when it starts to dim or shut down.

"GOOD GENES ARE NICE, BUT JOY IS BETTER!"[1]

The longest-running study on happiness is an eighty-four-year-old study on adult development led by Harvard researchers.[2] They discovered that having a happy childhood, what we would call a childhood filled with joy and appreciation, was correlated with better physical health, strong relationships later in life and a lower likelihood of depression by the age of thirty. Robert Waldinger, the current director of this study, reports, "Good relationships keep us happier and healthier."[3]

Researchers looked at what ingredients go into a healthy, happy life and discovered several important findings. First, a happy childhood gives us a foundation we will build on throughout our lives. Thankfully, they also found that a bad childhood can be turned around later in life when we actively grow joy habits.

Researchers noted that time with loved ones has a strong positive effect on well-being, so the quality of our relationships is more important than quantity. Robert Waldinger said, "Good relationships don't just protect our bodies; they protect our brains. And those good relationships, they don't have to be smooth all the time. Some of our octogenarian couples could bicker with each other day in and day out, but as long as they felt that they could really count on the other when the going got tough, those arguments didn't take a toll on their memories."[4]

How well we use coping strategies is important for helping us navigate turbulent times. We call these coping strategies the relational skills or habits that help us hold on to joy or return to joy when things go wrong. According to the research, there were at least three crucial factors to living a happy, satisfying life.

A healthy lifestyle. Habits like exercise, plenty of sleep, and good nutrition were common components of happy people.

Letting go of failure. Dwelling on past failures only keeps us discouraged and depressed rather than joyful and peaceful. The study showed that happy adults were better at letting go of past failures and focusing on the things that bring them joy.

Stable relationships. The most important finding, however, was that close relationships are the strongest predictor of happiness, more than anything else. Those who were most satisfied with their relationships at fifty years old were the healthiest by eighty years old. Waldinger went on to say, "Loneliness kills. It's as powerful as smoking or alcoholism."[5]

THE JOY GAME

We have mentioned before that five minutes in a state of joy can help quiet your brain and train it to amplify joy rather than fear. To help you practice getting your mind into a joyful place, we encourage people to play "the Joy GAME." GAME represents four practices to help us focus on what we have to appreciate.

G—Gratitude. The "G" of GAME stands for gratitude. In this sense we mean anything in our *present* situation worth appreciating. For me, at the moment, that is pretty easy. I am at a friend's house, sitting on a veranda with my daughter, sipping coffee, and looking across a valley at Pikes Peak on a picture-perfect day with not a cloud in the sky. We are enjoying a panoramic view of the Front Range that includes a clear view of the Garden of the Gods just a few hundred yards away. Of course, not every day is blessed with such a view. Sometimes we have to look a bit harder to find what there is to appreciate in our present situation. The goal, however, is not simply to list reasons to be grateful. The goal is to let yourself feel the experience in your body and to stay in that experience for a few minutes.

A—Anticipation. The "A" of GAME stands for anticipation. We have found it is always helpful to have something to anticipate with joy. For example, later today I will pick up my son from the airport. Later in the evening there is a basketball game I want to watch. Later in the week I'm going golfing. Having something you look forward to doing helps give us capacity to endure the hardship that often happens in between.

As we mentioned earlier, hope is often equated with having a plan. It hurts when we plan for something good to happen and those plans get ruined. It can tempt us to stop hoping and stop planning, but that would be a mistake. There is often more joy in the anticipation of what is coming than in the event itself. It would be a shame to rob ourselves of the joy of anticipating the good stuff to come.

M—Memories. The "M" of GAME stands for memories. We can relive past experiences that made us smile and brought us joy. Spending time in those memories is a great practice for developing the habit of appreciation. As I look at the mountains in front of me, I can think back to other trips where I have seen amazing natural beauty. Taking five minutes to relive one of those memories is a great way to calm ourselves down and build some joy at the same time. For example, if I close my eyes I can remember boarding a ferry to cross the Puget Sound from Seattle to the Olympic Peninsula in Washington. There was a cool breeze and I was with several friends from a conference I was at. The golden hour was just beginning, and it was a rare clear day that allowed us to see Mount Rainier rise in the distance in all its glory. As the sun set, the colors on the mountain changed from white to salmon to red to blue.

It probably took me three minutes to type that last paragraph, but taking the time to do it allowed me to live in that memory for a few minutes and revisit the joy. Sharing that memory with someone else who entered into the joy with me would just make the experience that much more powerful. Collecting joyful memories that we revisit on a regular basis is wonderful practice for growing our emotional capacity.

E—Experiences. The "E" of GAME stands for experiences. The idea here is to be creative and do activities or plan activities that we enjoy. For example, if I like gardening, making sure I plan to spend some time with my garden gives me something to anticipate, which hopefully becomes something that will help me feel gratitude in the present, and give me a memory to revisit later. There is almost no end to the experiences we can plan, but anytime we can share those experiences with someone else who also enjoys them, our joy will multiply. That is one of the nice things about joy. Sharing it with others doesn't rob us of any of our own joy, it simply makes it grow.

Throughout this book we have included exercises to help you grow your capacity for joy. Let us encourage you to take a few minutes right now to play the Joy GAME for five minutes and see if your body doesn't feel more relaxed.

THE FOUNDATION OF YOUR JOY HOUSE

The two habits of calming and appreciating are essential to the foundation of any joy house. It doesn't matter who you are, these two habits bring emotional stability to the foundation of our world. As we noted earlier, quieting is the number one predictor of long-term emotional health and appreciation is the fastest way to begin growing our capacity for joy.[6]

If you have been living with a fear house in your inner world, it is going to take some work to lay the foundation for a new house, but it is totally worth the effort. These two habits build resiliency. They allow you to roll with the punches life throws at you, so you can calm down as needed and restore joy when your levels get depleted. They train us with the skills we need to endure hardship well.

In the next few chapters we will talk about how to build on this foundation. For now, we want to introduce you to some exercises for building the habit of appreciation.

JOY WORKOUTS FOR APPRECIATION

Before we move on to the next two habits of building a joy house, we want to encourage you to go through the exercises that have already been introduced and to especially focus on building the habit of appreciation by doing the exercises in this chapter. It is amazing what five minutes here and there can do for our emotional health.

JOY WORKOUT #5—*Gratitude*

This exercise focuses on those joyful moments we are thankful for.

1. Take three minutes to reflect on a positive moment from the past twenty-four hours.
   a. This can be anything from an interaction to something you observed, heard, or experienced. It can be a moment in your day when you smelled freshly ground coffee beans, enjoyed seeing flowers in your yard, listened to birds singing, kicked off your shoes when you walked in the door of your house, or sank into your couch at the end of the day.

     b. The goal is to try your best to focus on the elements of this moment that were meaningful.

     c. Anytime you get distracted or your mind wanders, return to what was special in the memory.

2. Now give this moment a name.

3. Identify how you feel in your body and mind as you reflect on the positive aspects in this memory.

4. Next, take three minutes to reflect on a joyful moment from the past week.

     a. You can look at pictures on your phone if that helps to jostle a memory.

     b. The goal is to try your best to focus on the elements of this moment that are meaningful.

     c. Anytime you get distracted or your mind wanders, return to what was special in the memory.

5. Identify how you feel in your body and mind as you reflect on the positive aspects in this memory.

6. Now set a timer for ninety seconds. In your mind, go back and forth between the two appreciation memories as though you were looking out two windows. This may be more difficult than it sounds, but try your best to shift between the two appreciation moments while you focus on what is special in each memory.

7. Once the timer goes off, notice how you feel. Journal or type out your thoughts and observations on this exercise. Include whether this "two windows" practice was easy or difficult.

8. As you think about tomorrow using this lens of appreciation, what comes to mind about what you hope to see in terms of your experiences, expectations, relationships, thoughts, and feelings? Note: If you like, you can imagine a third window that is blank. What can you expect to see in this window as you reflect on the two appreciation windows?

9. Find a friend or family member to do this exercise with you, then review your answers, share your stories, and listen to your friend's thoughts and stories.

JOY WORKOUT #6—*Joy memories*

Practicing appreciation shifts our attention from fear to joy and peace. Appreciation generates feel-good chemicals that reward us for reflecting on the good stuff.

1. Find a comfortable place to sit and reflect on a favorite memory when you enjoyed a special meal with people.
   a. Give this moment a name.
   b. Identify how you feel in your body and mind as you reflect on this favorite meal moment.

2. Reflect on a time you received a gift that was meaningful for you.
   a. Give this moment a name.
   b. Identify how you feel in your body and mind as you reflect on this meaningful gift moment.

3. Reflect on a time you enjoyed the outdoors with a friend or family member.

    a. Give this moment a name.

    b. Identify how you feel in your body and mind as you reflect on this meaningful outdoor memory.

4. Find a friend or family member to review your answers, share your stories and listen to your friend's thoughts and stories.

5. Close by discussing what you notice after doing this exercise. Include a discussion about what you notice is the difference between reflecting on these moments on your own versus sharing and listening to stories with a friend.

JOY WORKOUT #7—*Experiences (appreciation increases joy)*

When we reflect on times of joy, what we call appreciation, we prepare ourselves for face-to-face joy that stirs hearts, brings smiles, and sets the stage for more joy. In this exercise, we use appreciation to share joy with someone special to us.

1. For this exercise you will need a friend or family member to practice with you.

2. Reflect on three qualities you enjoy in your friend.

3. Think of specific examples when you observed your friend use each quality.

4. Consider how this quality impacts you. In other words, share what happens in you when you see the quality in your friend.

   Example:

   a. Quality: *I enjoy that you are generous with your time and energy.*

   b. Example: *Remember last week when you stopped to help a woman at the grocery store who dropped her fruit in the aisle? I know you were in a hurry, yet you did this kind act.*

   c. Result: *Your generosity inspires me to be more generous and stay attentive to other people's needs!*

5. Now take turns sharing these thoughts with your friend. Be sure to include the quality you enjoy, the moment you saw this quality in action, and mention how this quality impacted you.

6. Finish the exercise by discussing the following topics:

   a. Share what you noticed while you practiced this exercise.

   b. What changed in your body and mind? How does it feel to reflect on and discuss these topics?

   c. What happens when you express appreciation to someone else?

   d. Is it easier for you to give or receive appreciation?

CHAPTER 5

Storytelling: Habit #3

I (MARCUS) ONCE GOT SO ANGRY with my baseball coach that I quit the team during my senior year of high school. I had just been thrown out at third base, which was a big mistake and I felt a lot of shame and anger. Rather than meeting me in my emotion and helping me calm down, my coach escalated the situation. In a fit of anger, I said, "If that's the way it is, I quit."

Not exactly a model of emotional maturity himself, my coach immediately accepted my impulsive offer. It was a mess. I was a senior and a team captain in my third year as a varsity player. In a moment, I had messed up everything. I suddenly felt remorse and then panic. I felt like I had just ruined my life. At that moment, I didn't have the maturity to act like myself and I didn't know how to return to joy. I felt my chest tighten and my face grow hot. Before I knew it, I found a quiet spot away from the team and started to sob.

This is not a story of successfully handling my emotions. It is a story that reminds me how I should have handled my emotions better. Once I calmed down, I apologized to the coach and we resolved things enough for me to stay on the team, but it likely damaged my opportunity at a college scholarship. He benched me for several games and, even though I missed a third of the season as a result, I was still voted second team all-conference.

Even now, I tend to take a deep breath when I tell that story, but it reminds me how important it is to handle our emotions well, and how we often make our problems bigger when we don't. No one is perfect. I regret what happened. But what happened that day has helped me learn the importance of not forgetting who I am when I get angry, and to take the time to get my emotions under control before I speak.

I (Chris) have a baseball story as well. I grew up playing baseball all my life. I played in grade school up to high school until my senior year. One day I got word that one of the younger players, the coach's son, was going to take my position. Even though I was a good player, I was going to lose my position for my senior year of high school. This was too much for my ego! I felt hurt and humiliated by this decision. I decided I wasn't even going to play. I gave up.

Where Marcus felt hot and angry in his example, I felt sad and hopeless. In spite of the coach's attempts to convince me to play my senior year, I refused and forfeited all opportunities to play college ball.

At the end of the day, we have to learn how to manage our emotions so we stay our relational selves under stress. Otherwise, the outcomes can be life-changing. Most of us have stories of reacting in some regrettable way. Like Marcus, we flew off the handle and lost it. Or, like Chris, we threw in the towel and gave up. When it comes to storytelling, we could tell these stories and end with the defeat and the regret. But we choose to tell the stories as lessons we have learned about the importance of returning to joy before we make life-changing decisions. How we tell our stories determines how we see ourselves and how we see the world.

HOW TO TELL A JOY STORY

A joy story explains how we faced a negative emotion in one of three ways.

1. We dealt with a hard emotion, but still acted like ourselves.
2. We dealt with a hard emotion, but were able to recover and return to joy.
3. We dealt with a hard emotion, but learned a helpful lesson even if we learned it the hard way.

Here are some keys you need to know about joy stories:

Talk about small or moderate emotions. Don't start with the worst thing that ever happened to you or the biggest example of an upset emotion you can remember.

Describe how your body felt when you were upset and how your body felt once you recovered.

If telling the story in person, make sure your face expresses the emotions you are feeling and make eye contact and use your whole body to tell the story. For example, you might make a face that says, "Yuck!" And you bend over holding your stomach to describe the disgust you felt. Or you might stick out your bottom lip in a pout and droop your shoulders to express sadness.

Keep the story brief. Two to three minutes is usually plenty of time.

Here is a basic outline you might use. It spells STEP to help you remember the steps needed for a good joy story.

Setting. Invite people into the setting. Are you at home? School? Work? Vacation? Where are you when this is happening?

Trigger. Explain what triggered the emotion.

Emotion. Give the emotion a name and explain it with both words and with nonverbal body language.

Point. Make your point. Explain how you acted like yourself or how you recovered or the lesson you learned.

We also recommend collecting joy stories about a

variety of emotions. We recommend having a collection of stories for each of the six core protector emotions we call the SADSAD emotions:

- Sadness
- Anger
- Disgust
- Shame
- Anxiety (Fear)
- Despair

We will explore these in more detail soon.

As you collect stories it can help to give them names. For example, here is a story about disgust that I (Marcus) call the "Chocolate Mousse Story."

Setting: Once when I was out to eat at a restaurant with a buffet, I noticed they had chocolate mousse as a dessert option. I love chocolate mousse, so I made a mental note to get some on my second trip to the buffet.

Trigger: When I got back to the table, I was feeling real excitement, just thinking about the flood of flavor I was about to experience. Then I took my first bite. I quickly grabbed a napkin and spit the vile food into it as quickly as I could. Instead of chocolate mousse, I had accidentally filled my plate with liver pate!

Emotion: I felt sick in my stomach and my mouth felt coated with something truly revolting. Nothing is quite as awful as liver when you are expecting creamy chocolate.

The feeling of disgust was overwhelming and I felt like gagging.

Point: My friends were looking at me with concern until I explained what had happened. Immediately, they all started laughing and I was soon sharing in their laughter. I realized that the disgust I felt wasn't the end of the world, and the taste in my mouth would soon go away. I was quickly able to find the real chocolate mousse and I left the restaurant with more than a meal. I left with a story to tell.

This is a joy story, not because the only emotion I felt was joy, but because an upsetting emotion became the doorway to relational joy.

THE AIRPORT STORY

Here is another joy story about a time Chris had to deal with an angry man at an airport. It is a bit more detailed, because it involves several emotions. See if you can spot them and how Chris handled each emotion.

One day my colleagues and I were returning home from a trip. It was late at night, and there was one more flight to board before we would be home. My friends and I were about to walk onto the airplane to find our seats when a flight attendant stopped us at the door. "I'm sorry," she said, "but the plane is full. You will have to walk over to that desk to rebook your flight for tomorrow."

We felt deflated by this news, but we took a deep

breath and picked up our bags. We turned to leave when suddenly a loud crash startled us. The sound of suitcases slamming the ground was followed by a litany of profanity and expletives from a passenger behind us. Here was someone who lost his joy! The man approached the attendant, leaned in and let loose with yelling and screaming. I felt my stomach twist into knots. Things were getting intense quickly.

While walking to the desk, I kept my eye on this enraged passenger. The man continued his tirade, only now he was moving from the flight attendant to other airline employees standing in the terminal. He would walk up, stand in their faces, and start screaming. The terminal was silent except for the deafening sounds of this irate passenger. My concern increased for the man and the people he blasted. Within moments, my friends and I were in line waiting for assistance to rebook our flights for the next morning.

I watched as the furious fellow approached where we were standing. I was feeling sadness and some fear seeing the field of debris left in his wake. It was about this time a worrisome thought popped into my mind. I felt the sudden urge to go pray with this man. While I was a praying fellow, I felt resistance to this thought. "If I get close to this guy, he's going to knock me out!" I thought. My body tensed more while my heart raced.

While wrestling with the thought that I should pray

with this fellow, I noticed one of my colleagues staring at me. A grin formed on her face as she leaned in and whispered, "Chris, I think you are supposed to go pray with that man!" There was no getting out of it at this point. I decided I would approach this man and offer to pray with him, even if it killed me!

I walked over to where the man was standing. I could see his red face, sweaty forehead, and the pulsating veins in his neck. "Excuse me," I said. "I can see you are having a bad day, and I would be honored if I could pray for you." I braced myself, and my body tensed up expecting a violent outburst.

Much to my surprise, he had a bewildered look on his face. He nodded, then said, "Yeah. Okay. You can pray for me, I guess." I breathed a sigh of relief. We stood together as I gently placed my hand on his shoulder. We bowed our heads, and I prayed out loud so he could hear.

To this day, I have no idea what words flew out of my mouth, but I clearly remember the look on his face when I opened my eyes. I saw tears flowing down his cheeks. I was shocked at the sight. He turned to me then said, "You know, this is funny. I have been feeling like I need to get right with God." He went on. "I have recently been diagnosed with severe cancer. My time is short. I was on a trip to get medical help, and I'm on my way home to see my family. Not making that flight tonight means I lose precious time with my wife and daughters."

"Wow. There is a story here!" I thought. I felt sorrow for his situation. He then said to me, "Wait, I have to do something. I'll be back." He proceeded to walk away and go to every person he yelled at in that terminal. He apologized to all the people who felt like roadkill from his fury. It took some time because there were a lot of people!

The optics of this experience must have been riveting to onlookers. All eyes had been on this man who had so thoroughly changed the atmosphere in the airport terminal. He had popped the joy balloons of a lot of people, not just those he yelled at. Suddenly, a stranger interacted with him, they prayed together, and the man softened. Finding some joy, he proceeded to apologize to all the people he had offended. Because Chris had the ability to remain relational in the face of anger, anger actually became a doorway to relationship and helped bring peace to a situation that was spiraling out of control. Let's get the rest of the story from Chris.

The man returned from apologizing to the people he had offended, and we started talking. By this point I was feeling some joy. My face relaxed as the tension in my chest softened. I was glad he responded. He was relational and warm. He and I were both breathing deeply again! I introduced the man to my colleagues and said with a smile, "I don't think it is an accident you are here, because we are all stranded for the night. You are stuck with a group of counselors, pastors, and missionaries. We are all good listeners!" We spent time together that evening on our way to the hotel. I saw him the next morning at the airport with a smile on his face and a new Bible under his arm. He was gentle, kind, and warm as he interacted with people. Even though the man's circumstances were terribly painful, joy had been restored.

I often wonder what happened to that man. I wish I knew. What I do know is that this man found joy in the midst of his suffering. I'm pretty sure it changed his life. He gained an important story to share with his family and friends.

In this story we see a man who lost all ability to act like himself because of overwhelming emotions. Chris served as a mature guide who was able to meet the man in his emotions and help him remember who he was. As a result he was able to act like himself—a kind and gentle person who valued repairing broken relationships. Chris's ability to remain relational in the face of the explosion taking place also made this man's anger a doorway to relational connection rather than isolation.

REVIEWING THE AIRPORT STORY

So, were you able to spot the emotions? Here is what Chris embedded in this story.

Sadness. He felt deflated. But he handled it by taking a deep breath and acted like himself by staying relational with his group and starting to make other plans. Chris also expressed sadness (sorrow) over the mess that was being created.

Fear. First, Chris felt concern at the mess created by the angry man. Then his fear escalated when he felt like he was supposed to intervene. The idea of praying with an angry man was counterintuitive and scary.

Anger. The anger in this story was not something Chris felt. It was the emotion in the room he needed to confront. In this case, he confronted that emotion with kindness and relational connection.

Notice that the story has a title—"The Airport Story"—and it follows the STEP pattern.

Setting: The story takes place in an airport with a group of tired travelers late at night.

Trigger: An angry man creates a scene by yelling at people who clearly have no ability to correct the problem.

Emotion: Concern gives way to fear as Chris feels led to intervene. Fear made Chris breathe rapidly and his heart raced.

Point: The point of the story was to show how remaining relational allowed Chris to connect with a teammate, act like himself by helping, and offer a pathway to relationship to the angry man. The point is reinforced by the man's response. He returned to joy and regained his ability to remain relational and act like himself.

MAKING YOUR POINT—THREE OPTIONS

When it comes to making our point while telling a joy story, there are three primary options from which we can choose. (1) We can explain how we felt the emotion but still remained relational and acted like ourselves. (2) We can explain how the emotion triggered us so that we temporarily stopped acting like ourselves but were able to recover. (3) We can explain how we blew it completely, but learned a lesson from the experience.

Option 1: Stories about how we act like ourselves

Joy stories acknowledge that we all have weaknesses and face difficult emotions. The point isn't to celebrate how mature we are, but to remind ourselves and others of what maturity looks like even when emotions are running high.

Acting like ourselves refers to being the best version of ourselves. Too often we focus on who we are when the worst version of ourselves gets triggered. Learning to tell joy stories in which we feel hard emotions but still act like the best version of ourselves helps to reinforce our true identity.

There is more to us than what we do wrong. Sometimes we tell stories about our most cringeworthy moments, and conclude that we are bad people. Instead, we need to tell those stories and realize that a better version of ourselves was possible. There are times we temporarily forget who we are. We say and do things we wish we could take back. Our emotions often cause us to speak and behave in hurtful ways so that we do not live according to our values.

There is more to us than what we do wrong.

Acting like ourselves means we stay relational while we feel the emotion. We respond as we would if we were feeling joyful and peaceful. We continue to reflect the priorities and values that are important to us while we feel upsetting emotions. We behave in ways that reflect our character and personality. So, by acting like yourself in an emotion you behave in a way that is satisfying.

Option 2: Stories about how we recover to joy and peace

The expression "returning to joy" can sound like we stop feeling upset or overwhelmed and suddenly feel happy again. However, the phrase does not refer to the end of a negative emotion. It refers to recovering our ability to be glad to be with someone *in spite of* the emotion. When we get triggered, our relational self disappears and we act like someone else. Returning to joy is the process of getting our true self back online. This happens when we can find joy with another person even though our emotions are still upset.

I (Marcus) was once so upset with my wife that I shut

down and stopped talking to her. In fact, I had lost all ability to act like myself. She sat on the bed and I sat on the couch and we were both frustrated. It was a familiar experience. This time, however, she decided to put into practice some new skills we had learned. She realized I was shut down, so instead of pushing my buttons further, she asked if she could sit next to me. I shrugged my shoulders as if to say, "Suit yourself." She came over to the couch and sat close. Then she said, "Can I hold your hand?" I thought she was nuts, but reluctantly agreed. When I reached over and took her hand I could feel all of the energy in my body change. It was like a switch in my brain got flipped. I remembered that I liked this woman and that it was like me to keep the relationship bigger than the problem. Because of the way she handled the situation, we were able to have a productive conversation that ended with us happy to be together.

Learning to stay our relational selves is an important skill, but our brain also has to learn how to recover when we feel upset. Let's be real, it's no fun to stay stuck in unpleasant emotions with no path back to joy! Returning to joy and peace means making the shift from the back of our brain where we isolate ourselves when things go wrong to the front of our brains where our relational self resides.

When we share these recovery stories we describe what the upset was like and how it felt, then we focus on the shift back to joy and how this joy feels in our body and mind.

One day I (Chris) was working in the master bedroom when I heard a loud crash in my young son's bedroom down the hall. I opened the door to see water cascading over the edge of the sink in his room, as my son had decided it was a good idea to build a makeshift waterfall. My first instinct was anger at the mess. My body was tense. My brow furrowed. My mind was racing and my breathing was shallow. Then I quickly noticed my son was crying. He hurt himself, which brought some fear that he might have hurt himself badly. I ran over to turn off the water, then I took a deep breath as I bent down to check on him. I felt compassion for my child. It was clear he was upset. By this time my anger faded away and I felt tender toward my son. I was glad to be with him even in the midst of this watery mess we were sitting in!

If I had not returned to joy in this scenario, I might have reacted out of anger or even fear which would have made the situation worse. Instead, I was able to take a deep breath, pick up my young son, and comfort him. I felt relieved to hold him in my arms. "Daddy's here!" I said as I rubbed his back. I affirmed that this was frightening for him and once he calmed down, we dealt with the mess. While I felt sad for the glorious mess in his bedroom, I was glad he wasn't seriously injured. I was thankful we were together in this situation. We returned to joy.

Too often, situations like this escalate into unnecessary pain and trauma because we don't take a few moments to calm down and return to joy before we act.

Option 3: Stories of lessons learned

We all wish we could have do-overs in life. These are moments in which we handled a situation or feeling in a way that caused us to temporarily lose track of who we are. We say and do things that later make us cringe. Thankfully, even our mistakes are not in vain. We can use these situations where we failed to stay ourselves as an opportunity to update our brains with a better example by reimagining what could have been.

In these "do-over stories" we share how we dropped the ball and failed to stay ourselves. We then interject with a vision for how we would have wanted to handle the situation. We say, "If I could redo this moment, I would say this and do that instead." We take that approach to better capture our values and character and include how we would have wanted to handle a particular moment of weakness or temporary forgetfulness.

To effectively tell these do-over stories we paint a picture of the situation by including a description of what happened, where we messed up, and what we could have done differently. This kind of story engages our brain's identity center to simulate how we could have handled the situation better in some way. It uses our "as if" circuits in the brain to demonstrate how to stay ourselves and recover when feeling emotions and navigating circumstances that are demanding, painful, triggering, and simply too intense.

A NOTE TO NARCISSISTS

Perhaps this is a good time to say something about image management. We are not telling people to spin stories to make themselves look good. In fact, it is important to be honest about our failures and shortcomings. One of the most important skills we need to learn is how to feel shame without deflecting it to someone else.

We are all born narcissists. None of us is born handling shame well. It is a skill we must develop as we mature. We learn to handle shame when someone is not glad to be with us, but they stay relational with us. We learn that shame is not the end of the world. Joy is around the corner. *Yet we all do narcissistic things now and then. That doesn't mean we are all narcissists.* However, we need to be careful not to justify our actions and blame others for problems we helped create. Throwing other people under the bus is a specialty most people who struggle with shame learn to master.

Joy stories can be a great tool for helping us learn what it looks like to handle shame well. In many ways, the whole purpose of collecting joy stories is to train ourselves how to handle difficult emotions well, whether it is shame or something else.

BUILDING A JOY HOUSE

Hopefully, you have not only been reading this book, but you have started doing some of the exercises to help build your own joy house. I once asked a friend to endorse another book I had written about emotional resilience and growing joy. He agreed and wrote something like this: "Reading this book won't help you at all. But doing the exercises in it will change your life." He had a point. It is relatively easy to explain the importance of joy. It is much harder (and much more important) to actually build it. We might title a book (with apologies to Joel Osteen) *Your Best Life . . . Takes Work.*

In the next chapter, we are going to look at seven core emotions and how learning to tell stories about these specific emotions can help us grow our resilience so that we can bounce back from them more easily. In our experience, people who develop tracks for recovering from these specific emotions have the foundation they need for dealing with all of the others. Let's practice some exercises first.

JOY WORKOUTS FOR STORYTELLING

Learning to tell good stories about how we deal with our emotions helps us build a library of memories to guide us as we deal with our emotions in the future. Here are three Joy Workouts to help you develop your ability to tell the kind of joy stories taught in this chapter.

JOY WORKOUT #8—*The STEP sequence for joy*

For this exercise we use the STEP sequence to share joy and show an example about a time we remained relational.

1. Think about a time you felt some glad-to-be-together joy with other people. Identify the ways you remained relational in this story.
   a. Did you interact with people?
   b. Did your face, voice, and words convey joy?
   c. Were you attentive and present with others?
   d. What else did you say or do to stay relational with others?
2. Now use the STEP sequence to prepare your story.
   a. Setting: Describe the setting for your story.
   b. Trigger: Explain what triggered your joy. Be specific about the interactions and details that made this a joyful experience for you.

    c. Emotion: Think through how you can use words to describe the joy you felt. Include nonverbal signs you can convey to demonstrate this joy to your listener. This would be your face, voice tone, gestures, movements and so forth. Capture what the joy looks like, sounds like and feels like.

    d. Point: Focus on how you stayed relational and handled this situation in a way that best reflects your character and personality.

3. Now that you have prepared your story, find a friend or family member and share your joy story. Include each STEP ingredient in your story.

4. Ask your friend what it was like listening to your story. What did your friend notice or observe while you shared your joy story?

5. Now invite your friend to practice the exercise and prepare a joy story using the STEP ingredients.

JOY WORKOUT #9—*The STEP sequence with emotions*

For this exercise we use the STEP sequence to show how we found joy after an upset. This is a time where an unpleasant emotion became the doorway to relational joy. The goal is to use a low to moderate level of emotion, nothing too intense. We pick something that is simple and manageable to show how we returned to joy from one of the SADSAD emotions. Keep the story concise, between two to three minutes. Try to avoid loss in your story in order to avoid triggering loss in your listener.

1. Think about a time you felt some minor upset and you returned to glad-to-be-together joy with other people. Contrast the moment you were upset with the moment you returned to joy in the story.

Example: *I was angry when I asked my son to stop playing with the dog and getting her riled up so she would bark wildly and loudly in the house while my wife was on the phone. My son did not listen and kept going with the unwanted behavior. My face became hot. I felt my stomach tighten while my chest and shoulders tensed. My focus was on stopping this behavior! However, I paused to take a breath and inhaled slowly and deeply through my nose. I could feel the air go deep in my lungs as my stomach stretched out with each breath. I walked over and knelt by my son. My anger began to lessen. In a calm voice I said, "I see you are having fun playing with the dog. However, did you hear what I asked you to do?" He looked up and nodded in agreement. I reached out to touch his shoulder and said, "I like seeing you have fun with the dog, but when I ask you to stop and you don't stop, I quickly lose my joy with you. What needs to happen here?" He hung his head and said, "I'm sorry, Dad. I was having fun and did not want to stop. I will work on listening better." Together we returned to joy as a smile broke out on my face and I gave him a hug saying, "Thank you." What could have been a pothole turned into a minor speed bump. We were now grinning as energy returned to our faces. The anger left my body as I felt calmer. I could breathe easier and my shoulders relaxed while my chest deepened with each breath.*

2. Now use the STEP sequence to prepare your story. Keep each step simple so your story stays concise.

    a. Setting: Describe the setting. What important details provide some context?

    b. Trigger: Explain what triggered your upset. Be specific about the interactions and details that made this an unpleasant experience for you.

    c. Emotion: Think through how you can use words to describe the upsetting emotion you felt as well as the joy. Include nonverbal signs you can convey to demonstrate this bridge from the upset back to joy. Use your face, voice tone, gestures, movements and so forth. Capture what the upset looked like, and then show the joy.

    d. Point: Focus on how you felt upset but you returned to joy. We want to emphasize the ways the upset led to relational joy.

3. Now that you have prepared your story, find a friend or family member to share your joy story with. Include each STEP ingredient in your story.

4. Ask your friend what it was like listening to your story. What did your friend notice or observe in you while you shared your story? Did your friend feel the upset in your story, as well as the joy?

5. Invite your friend to practice the exercise and prepare a return-to-joy story using the STEP ingredients.

JOY WORKOUT #10—_The STEP sequence for lessons learned_

We use the STEP sequence to share an example where we temporarily forgot who we were. We reacted in some way. This is a do-over story to share a time we did not handle a situation or emotion well and we would like to replay it again and come up with a redo example. Keep your story simple and concise, between two to three minutes if possible.

1. Think about a time you were upset and did not handle a situation well. Identify how you would like to have a do-over and do something differently.

   Example: *I became upset with my child because she did not clean up her room like I asked. I was mad. In my upset, I grounded her and dished out consequences and punishments. I overreacted with my intensity and emotions. I regret this. If I could go back and try this again, I would calm down first before doling out consequences. I would give her the opportunity to explain herself. I would ask her what she thinks the consequences should be. I would stay relational and talk this through instead of reacting harshly. We would discuss the consequences only after I calmed down. Quieting and resting before talking would have been much more satisfying.*

2. Now use the STEP sequence to prepare your story. Keep each step simple so your story stays concise.

    a. Setting: Describe the setting for your story. What important details provide some context?

    b. Trigger: Explain what triggered your upset. Be specific about the interactions and details that made this a difficult experience.

    c. Emotion: Think through how you can describe the feelings and emotions you felt. Include the nonverbal signs you can convey to demonstrate your feelings and experiences. This would be your face, voice tone, gestures, movements, and so forth.

    d. Point: Focus on how you would like to go back and redo the experience. Highlight lessons you learned and what you would say and do differently in a way that reflects your character and values.

3. Now that you have prepared your story, find a friend or family member and tell your lessons learned story. Include each STEP ingredient in your story.
4. Ask your friend what it was like listening to your story. What did your friend notice or observe in you while you shared your story?
5. Invite your friend to practice the exercise and prepare a story using the STEP ingredients.

CHAPTER 6

Maturity and the Big Six Protector Emotions

WE LIVE IN A CULTURE that is big on making good choices. But when it comes to dealing with our emotions, choices alone aren't going to get the job done. There is a pretty basic reason for this. Our choices are limited by our capacity. For example, my son was an offensive lineman in college. I am forty years older than him and I played tennis in college. His capacity to lift weights is so much greater than mine, it isn't funny. Because of his capacity, he can choose to work out with well over two hundred pounds on the bar when he goes to the gym. On the other hand, it has been thirty years since that was an option for me. In the same way, when it comes to regulating our emotions, our choices are limited by our capacity to handle the weight of those emotions.

The ability to handle emotional weight is at the core of what it means to be mature. You can tell who the most mature person is in any setting, not by who has the most degrees or the highest status, but by who can handle the most emotional weight without being triggered.

The capacity to handle emotional weight is directly related to our personal maturity. For example, it is silly to ask a crying infant to calm down or control themselves, because that choice isn't even an option for them. They haven't developed the capacity to do that. We expect children to have more capacity and so we ask a bit more of them, but they need a lot of help. To be an adult implies that we have learned the skills and habits necessary to regulate our emotions and not be controlled by them.

Let's take a brief look at the five basic stages of maturity development and how they impact our ability to handle emotional weight.[1]

INFANT

An infant has no emotional capacity. Every new emotion a baby feels is overwhelming. This is because the elements in the brain necessary for dealing with negative emotions are largely undeveloped at birth. Infants are completely dependent on someone with more developed maturity to regulate their emotions for them. Thus, we cuddle and coo and soothe and sing and rock and talk in a way that we hope will help them return to joy. If this happens over and over again, the baby will learn to feel safe and form secure attachments. If this does not happen, the baby's brain will not develop properly. The house in their inner world will become anchored in fear rather than joy. They will likely struggle with emotional instability for the rest of their lives.

If we reach our adult years without receiving the infant-level training we needed, we may find that we still handle many of our emotions like an infant. For example, we may fuss and whine and pout about our problems because we never learned how to ask for what we need. The skill of asking for what we need is a child-level skill. If certain emotions keep us from doing that, it is a clue that we are stuck in infant-level maturity. Think of the grandfather whose coffee runs out and he simply grunts and rattles his mug, fully expecting that someone else will notice what is wrong and take care of it for him. He doesn't say, "Will someone please get me more coffee?" Instead, he lets people know he is upset and expects them to fix the problem, because even though he may be over seventy years old, he is demonstrating infant-level maturity.

Emotional infants are good at letting people know they are upset. They get angry easily. They tend to be addicted to non-relational substances like drugs or alcohol and to non-relational experiences like masturbation, constant entertainment, or the adrenaline rush that comes from fear. It is important to state that most people are

> *Emotional infants are good at letting people know they are upset.*

not stuck in infant-level maturity because they choose to be there. They are stuck because they missed out on something they needed in order to develop that maturity when they were the age to do it easily. If we want to grow our emotional maturity and live with greater joy, we need to admit where we are and start working on the skills we missed.

CHILD

A child normally has more capacity than an infant. Their brains are more developed, so it takes more to overwhelm them. They also have more skills and more experience in dealing with strong emotions. One of the primary tasks that needs to be mastered by the time we reach our childhood years is learning to regulate emotions. We do this by being with people who can do it when we are upset and, over time, we learn to identify how we feel and how big our emotions are. Children learn to "use their words" when they are upset and ask for what they need.

If all goes well, I will reach my adult years with a well-developed joy house in my inner world. Joy will be the default setting in the way I live so that when I am upset, I can recover and return to joy. If I have learned to live out of my joy house as a child, I will be positioned for success as an adult. However, if trauma interrupts my development, I may find myself entering my adult years still living in a house of fear. As a result, I will have fewer relational skills and less capacity to handle life's challenges. The lack of a joy foundation will make me want to avoid becoming an adult. I will resist responsibility!

In order to grow their emotional maturity, children need adults to validate their emotions, comfort them, and help them recover. And this needs to happen over and over again. Suppose a child is out playing on the sidewalk and has an accident in which they bang their knee on the cement and start to bleed. Such an experience is apt to produce a lot of fear. They are not used to seeing blood come out of their body. They don't know just how bad this might be and it really hurts—maybe worse than anything they can remember. So the child runs home, crying and upset.

Let's suppose Mom is there to meet the child. How Mom responds to this situation is going to have a big impact on the child's maturity development. Ideally, the mother would validate the child's emotions. She might bend down to look the child in the eyes and show on her face that she can see how much this hurts and how scary this is. Once she meets the child in their big emotions, she begins to comfort the child. "Don't worry," she might say, "You aren't in trouble and this isn't too bad. Let me wash this off and put a Band-Aid on it." By validating the big emotions and making the problem smaller, she helps the child manage the situation and recover. The more this happens, the more fully developed the joy pathways in the child's brain will become.

Of course, we probably all know parents who don't handle this situation with quite as much maturity. Some ignore the child and keep watching television or play on their phone. Some get angry at their kid for creating an inconvenience. Some merely slap on the Band-Aid and never address the emotions. What a child doesn't get in moments like this can be thought of as A Trauma, and it stunts their maturity development.

If we enter the adult world without mastering these significant child-level skills, we will find ourselves routinely overwhelmed by the demands of life. People who are stuck at child-level maturity learn to fear negative emotions and resist doing hard things. The more emotions they instinctively avoid, the smaller their world becomes.

ADULT

People with adult-level maturity have mastered all the infant- and child-level skills needed to tend to their own emotions. This doesn't mean we never get overwhelmed. It means moderate-level, negative emotions don't make us blow up, shut down, or melt down. But those stuck at infant- or child-level maturity who are trying to navigate an adult world can find themselves constantly living on the edge of their capacity.

In a sense, we can think of adults as people who have learned to live on the fuel of joy. They have a well-built joy house and can return to a place of internal peace and joy on a regular basis. Because they have developed the four habits of joy-filled people, they have enough joy strength to endure hardship well. As a result they are stable and relational—the kind of people who keep relationships bigger than problems and handle big emotions without turning into a different person.

We can think of adults as people who have learned to live on the fuel of joy.

If you are not sure what we mean by "turning into a different person," think of a person in your world who is normally a kind person, but who gets scary when they become angry. They may say, "You won't like me when I get angry." This is essentially an admission of emotional immaturity. Immature people often change their personality depending on the emotion they feel. Others tend to walk around them on eggshells because of it. One of the characteristics of adult-level maturity is the ability to act like ourselves even under stress.

The world needs more adults. We need more people who are running on the fuel of joy and handling their emotions with predictable stability. When we enter the role of parent without adult-level maturity, things can get overwhelming pretty fast. But if we have been living like an adult for several years, taking the next step to become a parent who finds joy in training our children is still challenging, but it feels more like an adventure than a burden.

PARENT

Parent-level maturity means I give life. I can take care of myself and sacrificially take care of my children at the same time. A parent is a life-giver (as opposed to a life-drainer). A parent doesn't just teach a child to obey or master the skills needed for school. A parent guides a child in the art of living. When our world is filled with parent-level people, it means there are a lot of people around who are not easily overwhelmed and have learned how to navigate the ups and downs of life with confidence, creativity, and resiliency.

Parents with well-built joy houses in their inner world have greater ability to enter into all of the big emotions their children face, deal with their own big emotions, and still find their way back to a place of calm and appreciation at the end of the day. Parenting is still hard. It still demands a lot of sacrifice. But parents whose inner world is anchored in joy will navigate those challenges with greater resilience than those whose inner world is built on fear. Parents confidently protect, serve, and enjoy their families.

ELDER

Elders are people whose children have become adults. Decades of navigating the challenges of parenting have grown their capacity to handle more emotional weight. As a result, elders often add value simply by their emotional stability. It takes a lot to overwhelm them. They stay relational during trials and remind people who they are in tough times. Elders bring the wisdom that can only be earned by enduring many hardships well and recovering when things go wrong.

People at elder-level maturity are often good at seeing the holes that need to be filled, both in the people they meet and in the communities they serve. They often make great surrogate parents or simply good friends who help the rest of us bear the weight of life. Some people spend a significant part of their lives as elders. Those years will be much more satisfying with a secure and stable joy house in the inner world.

A culture filled with mature elders is truly blessed. These individuals help bring stability to the entire community. They excel at facing the challenges of life without losing their joy. They also excel at helping those around them face hardship with grace. Businesses, schools, families, and churches all benefit from the presence of people with elder-level maturity.

THE PROTECTOR EMOTIONS

Now that we looked at capacity and maturity, this brings us to a closer look at the six motivations our brain uses when we have not mastered the skills to return to joy from our upsets. These are often called "protector" emotions because they are intended to protect us from pain. In this sense, each emotion serves a good purpose. They are not bad emotions, per se. However, they can become harmful when we don't regulate them.

The Life Model has identified six core protector emotions that we remember with the acronym SADSAD.[2]

- Shame
- Anger
- Disgust
- Sadness
- Anxiety/Fear
- Despair

Navigating these emotions is often easier if we understand something about them.

Shame

Brain science tells us positive looks from the parent are the most vital stimulus for the growth of the socially healthy, emotionally intelligent brain.[3] The brain doubles in size during the first year of life, and central to this developmental process is the presence of joy. Face-to-face joy is powerful! Joyful interactions help the brain grow and thrive. Joy is most centrally located in the left eye. Infants will seek out the mother's left side of her face because it's more expressive with emotions,[4] specifically the left eye because the brain's joy center is based in the right hemisphere's orbitofrontal region, the prefrontal cortex that's on the right side of the brain.[5] Infants will look to the eyes to find joy more than anywhere else on the mother's face, specifically the left eye since that shares information from the right hemisphere. (The right eye shows more information about thoughts from the left hemisphere.)

Since joy grows with glad-to-be-together glances, shame can be thought of as anti-joy, because we are not bringing someone joy in a given moment. The face is not lighting up to see us! As little kids who are used to seeing Mommy and Daddy light up with delight when we are around, it can be overwhelming when we see their faces telling us we are not bringing them joy. Perhaps we drew pictures on the wall with crayons and Mommy isn't very happy with me. That feeling of shame is something all of us need to learn how to experience and still act like ourselves. When infants do not learn to process shame and find joy from this feeling, they eventually avoid shame or even sidetrack from shame to other more manageable emotions like anger or sadness. We can spend our entire lives running from these feelings we don't know what to do with!

When we feel shame, we feel like hanging our heads and avoiding eye contact. It saps our bodies of energy. Toxic shame is what happens when people misuse the corrective measures of healthy shame and weaponize the emotion. Toxic shame happens when the narrative that gets attached to the emotion tells us we are "bad." Toxic shame attacks our identity and makes us feel like we are the problem, rather than our behavior needing some correction.

Shame can be thought of as anti-joy.

Everyone feels shame at various times to varying degrees, so we all have to learn how to feel shame without turning into a different person. One of the reasons for telling joy stories related to shame is to give our brain a clear picture of what it looks like to handle the emotion like an adult so we can feel it but not be overwhelmed by it. If we get skilled enough, we can even use shame to create a doorway for relational connection to others. Let's see how Chris managed shame from the time he was a source of upset with his friends.

One day I was following a car filled with several friends of mine. We were driving to the office where we all worked. On the way, I turned a corner and saw my friends pulled over to the side of the road. Assuming they were waiting to tell me something, I pulled up next to them.

While pulling up, I could see their faces turned back my way. They were looking outside the car window. They were obviously thrilled about something, but I had no idea what it was. About the time I was close to their car, I saw their faces shift from joy and delight to fear and panic. Out of the corner of my eye I saw something in the road near the front left tire of my car.

We all have to learn how to feel shame without turning into a different person.

It was too late. As my car lurched forward, I heard the awful sound of my car running over something hard. I watched as my friends' faces turned to horror, then disgust. "Oh no!" I thought to myself, "I think I just ran over a turtle!" Yep. I did. I ran over the lovely turtle they had stopped to admire.

My friends let out a loud "YUUUUCK!" They were disgusted by what they just witnessed, both the loss of a precious turtle as well as the manner of this unfortunate loss.

They looked up at me with revulsion and confusion. I was the source of their distress! I felt my stomach tighten. A weight came over my chest and shoulders. My face flushed. I felt physically sick thinking about what just happened. Between the sound of the turtle and the look on their faces, I felt terrible. Because of me they had to endure this awful scenario. I wanted to run and hide! I wanted to go back in time and have a do-over.

I profusely apologized. I let the group know I did not realize they were pulled over to see a turtle. They looked at me and listened. They gave an understanding nod then uttered something along the lines of, "Okay; we will see you at the office." On the drive over I took some deep breaths to calm down. I felt intense shame. My mind replayed the incident and the expressions on their faces. Even though this was an accident, I felt guilty. When I arrived at the office, I gave my friends a big hug, then apologized again for the terrible ordeal. I shared my thoughts that I believed they were waiting for me to pull up.

Thankfully, they could see my perspective, and were gracious and understanding about the situation. They could tell I was feeling bad. They said, "We know you, Chris, and we know you would never do this intentionally. You love animals!"

I felt understood by their words. I could feel more relaxed, seeing their faces soften. Receiving their attunement was refreshing. Some even started joking with me and gave me a hard time about being a "turtle killer." I was feeling lighter, more relieved, and glad to be with my friends once again. We all felt sad for the loss of this innocent turtle, but within a short amount of time the shame faded as joy and peace increased. I could breathe easier as the tension left my body. My shoulders relaxed. I was glad I stayed relational with my friends. I helped them understand my perspective, and they listened. I could apologize for putting them through this awful ordeal. In many ways, this brought us closer together.

Anger

Anger is the high-energy emotion that wants to make something stop. We want to end some pain we are feeling or stop some injustice from happening. Anger can flare when we feel like a goal is being blocked and we know whose fault it is. If I just want to spend a nice, quiet evening reading a book and my kids listen to loud music or play with too much enthusiasm, I might get angry at them when they really haven't done anything wrong. They just blocked my goal of a quiet evening and I need to make that stop!

Anger tends to make our breathing shallow and fast, our nostrils flare, our muscles tense, and our focus intensify. Joy stories help us remember how to feel anger and regain our composure before responding. They can also help us remember that I don't have to turn into a rage monster or a spoiled kid when I get angry. It is possible to remain an adult even when faced with this big emotion. Handling anger well can even strengthen relationships.

A friend of ours who served in the military tells of a time he got so angry at a fellow officer, he literally started seeing red (a sign that the blood pressure behind the eyes has gotten so intense that capillaries are breaking). This officer completely disregarded orders and was on the verge of creating a potentially catastrophic situation because of his disregard for diplomacy. They were on assignment in the former Soviet Union and the junior officer was arrogantly disregarding what he felt were paranoid instructions on how to conduct himself. It turned out there was no paranoia in the instructions. Our friend had to get his own emotions under control in order to handle himself well in that situation and attempt to minimize the damage. Later, he chastised the junior officer, but only after he first calmed down. He handled his anger in a way that increased the younger man's trust and strengthened their relationship.[6]

Disgust

Disgust is related to the feeling we want to vomit. It often triggers the gag reflex that makes us want to get something poisonous out of our system, but it can also get triggered by something repulsive that we don't want anywhere near us. Most parents have to learn to deal with disgust and still be relational when they change diapers. The odor often leads to a physical reaction in which we curl down the edges of our lips, pull back from the baby, and feel queasy in our stomachs. However, most of us can stick with it long enough to let the baby know we are still happy to be with them as we deal with the mess at hand. Chris has an example of disgust.

When I changed my son's diaper for the first time, I did not know what I was doing. He was only three days old, and let's just say I was unskilled and needed some practice. I had an idea of the steps from watching Jen, so I figured I could pull it off. While changing my son's diaper on the changing station one day, I lifted his legs high into the air, just above his head. At this moment my son was cooing and watching me closely while I interacted with him. It was a joyful moment until, without realizing it, the position of his legs pulled back in the air applied too much pressure to his belly. The angle and motion turned my child into a cannon. You probably know where this is going.

The pressure caused an explosion. Fecal matter flew across the room hitting the opposite wall. I let out a loud cry, "Oh nooo!" The disgust was palpable. I gasped at the sight, the sounds, and the smells. I felt my nose curl. My face tightened with disgust. My eyes were squinting and I tried to inhale very slowly to avoid breathing in the noxious air. I wanted to run away! I noticed my son watching me. He seemed curious at all the fuss, but he was clearly enjoying the moment. I stayed relational. I grabbed some wet wipes while holding on to my son's legs and we locked eyes while I cleaned up what I could reach. I used my voice tone to convey that I was still glad to be with him while my face was still stuck in feeling disgust. I interacted with him and I felt my face start to shift from disgust to some joy to be with him. I then spoke in a high tone, telling him what I was doing while I was cleaning. Soon, I called for reinforcements from both Jen and my mother-in-law while I continued to interact with my son.

Once he was cleaned and in new clothes, we played and snuggled together. Joy was present as I held him on my lap. My body was relaxed; my mind, calm. I felt lighter! I smiled as we made funny sounds together. I was genuinely feeling disgust at first, but I stayed relational, which is acting like myself. We ended up in a place of joyful, glad-to-be-togetherness that was a relief. To this day, "the cannon story" is a favorite tale my two sons want to hear.

As researchers study disgust, people who were exposed to foul smells tend to disapprove of other people more so than when they are in a neutral environment. Disgust is not only about things that are gross or nauseating. We often have to learn to deal with disgust for incompetence or perceived incompetence. There is a reason the people who made the Pixar movie *Inside Out* decided to make its representation of disgust a teenage girl whose attitude toward everything was basically, "Yuck. Get away from me."

Sadness

We feel sad when we lose something that brought us joy. Sometimes sadness can create a means of connecting. When I don't feel overwhelmed by your sadness and am actually happy to be with you despite your sadness, we can find joy together even if your sadness doesn't go away completely. Chris shares a sad story.

I had a favorite restaurant growing up that my parents would often take me to after we played racquetball at the gym. We would drive by and pick up tacos. The tacos were the best I've ever had. One day, I drove to the restaurant on my lunch break at work. I noticed the parking lot was empty. Upon closer inspection, I saw a "Closed" sign hanging in the window and on the sign read "Out Of Business."

"What? How could this be? They were always so busy," I said to myself. I felt deflated by this news!

This realization brought great sadness. I felt the energy leave my body. My shoulders hunched forward. I sighed and shook my head. I felt sadness cover my body like a thick blanket. I was feeling discouraged and disappointed. Yet I stayed relational in my sadness. I called my parents. I shared the sad news with them. Even though this was a disappointing moment, it was like me to stay relational when I feel this kind of sadness. It is like me to recognize that I feel sad and not try to fight it. Later that day, I told my friends about this news. I shared some of my favorite stories about this restaurant, the tasty tacos, and the wonderful workers who served me over the years. Even though I felt heavy about the situation, I stayed relational and found joy reflecting on the good things I liked about the restaurant. I felt thankful for the years of service. My attitude shifted. I felt like I was given a gift over the years instead of feeling like something was stripped away from me. We try to tell stories that aren't too intense so the sadness does not lead to attachment pain, the pain of loss and death. We will discuss attachment pain shortly, but this kind of pain makes it difficult for the brain to stay relational. Attachment pain is when we talk about the loss of a pet, the death of a loved one, or the abandonment of a child. Avoiding these "hot topics" keeps our stories within a manageable range. Here is the reason why Chris told a story about tacos instead of the time his dog was hit by a car or when his grandfather passed away.

Fear and anxiety

Technically, fear and anxiety are different emotions. Fear is a reaction to potential danger and is triggered in the relational right hemisphere of the brain. Anxiety is anchored in imagination and is born in the logical left hemisphere of the brain. When I feel anxiety, I experience feelings of fear out of anticipation of what might happen or what feels inevitable.

Like anger, fear is a high-energy emotion. But instead of making us want to fight and stop something painful, fear makes us want to flee and get away from whatever has triggered us. Like all of these emotions, fear is not a choice we make. Fear is a reaction to an experience we have. As people have often noted, courage is not the absence of fear, but the ability to act like ourselves in the presence of fear. Chris has a fear story for us.[7]

One day I was driving down the road when a large hornet flew into my car. I was not clear where the hornet landed exactly, because I couldn't see where it was. I knew this much; it was the largest hornet I've ever seen! This situation made my heart race. I felt tension in my chest and tightness in my shoulders. My body was tight as I braced for an attack. My mind was racing with possible scenarios. My eyes darted searching for the hornet's whereabouts while I tried to stay on the road. I knew by this time the hornet was probably regaining his bearings, and would be unhappy to see me. I prayed for God to intervene!

Within moments, I pulled my car to the side of the road. In one swift motion, I opened the door and leaped out. The hornet flew away. I took some deep breaths. I could feel my body pulsating with adrenaline. As I took several deep breaths the tension started diminishing. I stretched out my arms and tried to loosen the tight muscles in my body. I thanked God I did not cause an accident while driving. I reflected on the moment and respected how powerful the fear reactions can be. I was also curious about what God was thinking when He made hornets! I was glad the ordeal was over, and my body felt peaceful once again. I enjoyed feeling calm and more relaxed.

Fear stories should paint a picture of the situation and include how we felt. We include our thoughts and body sensations, and we stay involved in the details so people understand our perspective.

Despair

Despair is directly related to hopelessness. I feel hopeless when there is no plan that can fix my problems with the time and resources at my disposal. One of the characteristics of maturity is the ability to remain emotionally stable even when we don't have the time, energy, or resources to get what we want. Chris has a despair example story.

In 2008 my wife, Jen, and I were preparing to run one of the largest conferences we've ever put on. Our excitement was high. We were less than a week out from the event, and I was playing church softball one evening. During the game I sprinted to catch a fly ball in the outfield. I wasn't going to reach it, so I dove to catch it. Unbeknownst to me, another fielder had the same plan. We collided midair. The crash was brutal. We lay sprawled on the grass moaning and groaning. When I came to, I was seeing stars. Once my eyes cleared I noticed my teammates standing over me. Sharp pain was shooting from my shoulder and arm. My head was throbbing. I was a wreck!

Paramedics took me to the hospital. I ended up with a concussion, dislocated shoulder, and a broken wrist. My bruised and battered body needed rest. There was just one problem. We were days away from the conference! I felt pressure to stay on top of the logistical needs I was responsible for managing. Yet, my mind couldn't hold on to details. Jen and I would walk into a store to make a purchase, and I would forget what I was supposed to buy. This happened several times where I forgot important details. My brain was not working well. My body was sore and tired. I felt foggy in my head. I could feel the hopelessness increasing with each day. How would I be useful to emcee and run this conference? How could I stay on top of the many details required to run this event? How could I endure the long days when I feel so weak? I lacked the energy and stamina to function for very long. In my despair, I wanted to stay in bed and sulk. I felt so helpless and powerless. My face felt like it was sagging. My voice was soft. My strength was sapped. It was hard to look up and face people. My hopelessness was consuming me and robbing my joy.

I asked for help from others and prayed for a miracle. I had a wonderful group of people around me who knew what was going on and filled in. The speakers were attentive and understanding. They took steps to support me in my limitations. It felt like friends were carrying me through. The conference ended up being one of our best events that people still talk about to this day. I felt loved. Supported. Encouraged. It was wonderful! By the end of the conference, I felt grateful for sharing my weaknesses and having a supportive and tender response from others. This was a time of joy. To this day, I look back on this time and remember the contrast of how desperate and hopeless I was feeling, yet how well things turned out.

Attachment pain

While the SADSAD emotions (shame, anger, disgust, sadness, anxiety/fear, and despair) can be thought of as protector emotions, there is another emotion that doesn't really protect from anything, it just hurts. That emotion is attachment pain. It is the deepest pain we can feel.

Attachment pain can be as fleeting as roaming an empty house looking for something to eat and not realizing that what we really want is some company. It can be incredibly intense when we want to be with someone desperately and simply can't be. They may be far away, emotionally distant, or perhaps the relationship has ended or they have died. Few things hurt as deeply as attachment pain.

> *Attachment pain can be as fleeting as roaming an empty house looking for something to eat and realizing that what we really want is some company.*

We want to use caution with attachment pain because this is the greatest pain the human brain knows. Loss, rejection, isolation, death, and abandonment cut deep. We want to pay attention to avoid attachment pain in our stories because it will activate attachment pain in our listeners. Yet we want to understand this pain so we have the language and the recognition to know when we hear it so we can use caution to avoid triggering attachment pain in others. This brings us to the steps for telling brain-friendly joy stories.

THE EMOTIONS WE NEED TO UNDERSTAND

There is no end to the emotions we can have because many times we are experiencing multiple feelings at the same time, or we may be feeling them at different levels of intensity. However, we can think of the protector emotions and attachment pain as something like a color wheel of negative emotions. Just as you can create nearly every color by combining white, black, red, blue, and yellow, so you can understand nearly every negative emotion as some shade, degree, or combination of SADSAD and attachment pain.

For example, shame spans a range that runs from mild embarrassment or awkwardness to intense feelings of worthlessness that can be utterly smothering. Toxic shame at this level can make you want to run and hide! In a similar way, anger can range from feeling frustrated or mildly upset to the compulsion of murderous rage. Some complex emotions, like dread and humiliation, are created by combining two or more of these core emotions. For instance, humiliation is what happens when shame and anger team up, while dread comes from a combination of fear and despair and can be made worse by additional emotions that blend over a period of time.

Each of these emotions can be triggered by beliefs (on the left side of the brain) or experiences (on the right side of the brain). Sometimes the feelings are reactions that come instinctively before we even think about them. Other times, they are the result of beliefs that may or may not be true. When emotions from our brain's cognitive engine are triggered by what we believe, we will need to do something about what we believe in order for the feeling to resolve. Information is helpful here.

If the feeling from our brain's emotional engine is triggered by an experience, it can shut down the upper levels of our brain's relational center before we even know what hit us. These are moments we end up thinking thoughts, saying words, and doing things we regret. Sometimes we are the last to know when these reactions show up!

In the next chapter we will look more closely at the battle for our thought life. We want to introduce you to some helpful tools for attacking toxic thoughts.

CHAPTER 7

Attack Toxic Thoughts: Habit #4

I (MARCUS) WALKED INTO a coffee shop one day and saw an advertisement for Alcoholics Anonymous on the bulletin board. It was promoting an event with some guest speakers, but what caught my attention was the phrase at the bottom of the flier in bold print: "Just ignore that committee in your head!" I had to laugh. Most of us know what it is like to have racing thoughts or to have arguments going on inside that we wish we could silence.

THE ROLE OF BELIEFS

Beliefs play a major role in our emotions. Sometimes our emotions trigger a flood of thoughts. At other times the flow moves in the opposite direction and our thoughts trigger a flood of emotions.

Let's say you get angry at your son for his bad attitude. The feeling of anger is often familiar. It isn't the first time you have felt this way, either about your son or about other people in your life. The emotion may trigger thoughts you have learned to think whenever you feel this way. You might think, "He always does this. His attitude always stinks. He's been this way forever. Why can't he see what this does to me? He's so selfish. I wish I could escape from here. I wish he'd learn some respect." Honestly, this may represent just a fraction of the barrage of thoughts that come cascading in when you feel this kind of anger!

This same process happens with nearly every emotion we feel. It can be exhausting. Sometimes we get depressed because our relationships or tasks feel hopeless. Sometimes we feel anxiety in our bodies and wonder what triggered it and if it will ever end. When big emotions combine, they create complex feelings that can feel like stepping on the accelerator and the brakes at the same time. Really big emotions can shut us down and get us stuck with the overwhelming thoughts in our heads.

Not only can emotions trigger a flood of thoughts, sometimes our thoughts can trigger a flood of emotions. If I believe someone is sabotaging me at work, I will react to that belief whether it is true or not. If I believe a certain politician is a horrible person with horrible policies, I may feel disgust and anger at the mere mention of that person's name, whether my beliefs are true or not. When I think of beliefs creating emotions that drive behavior, I often remember a night in junior high when I was at home playing with some friends. We had the music turned up and were playing a game when I looked across the room and saw a shadowy figure walk past the window. To make it worse, we were on the second floor of the house. Someone was walking around on the roof of our house looking for a window to climb in.

Immediately, my friends and I went downstairs and I did the only thing that made sense to me. I grabbed a baseball bat and went to the back door. When I got there, I saw a brown car I did not recognize parked in the driveway and I could feel my anxiety spike. I went outside and walked around to the side of the house, still holding my baseball bat. I looked up at the roof where I had seen the intruder. Sure enough, someone was up there trying to open a window. I yelled up at him and when he turned around I realized it was my older brother! Suddenly my emotions changed. I went from fear of someone breaking into my house to relief. "What are you doing up there?" I asked. He said he had been out with some friends (the brown car belonged to one of his buddies). He had come home and realized he didn't have his keys with him, so he knocked on the door and rang the doorbell but no one answered (apparently our music was too loud to hear him).

Suddenly, everything made sense. My new beliefs updated my emotions and with that, peace returned.

AUTOMATIC NEGATIVE THOUGHTS

Dr. Daniel Amen runs a series of brain clinics around the country and specializes in helping people determine what is happening in their brains that are driving unwanted emotions and behaviors. While we have not been to his clinics, we have been told that many of them have anteaters in the waiting room. Some also have pictures of anteaters or stuffed animals in the shape of anteaters decorating the office. They make pretty good conversation starters. After all, who goes to a medical office expecting to see anteaters? So it is not uncommon for people to ask, "What is up with the anteaters?" To which someone answers, "Glad you asked." Dr. Amen calls the flood of thoughts that accompany our emotions ANTS, which stands for Automatic Negative Thoughts.[1]

According to his website, Dr. Amen got the idea of ANTS (Automatic Negative Thoughts) after a particularly difficult day at the office.[2] He came home only to find a swarm of ants all over his kitchen floor. As he dealt with the problem it occurred to him that the swarm of ants mirrored the swarm of negative thoughts that often plagued his clients. His observation led to the idea that he needed to help his clients turn their brains into anteaters. The process worked so well, he was soon decorating his offices with anteaters.

We would agree with Dr. Amen that it is a great idea to turn our brains into anteaters. We need to learn some skills and strategies for winning the battle in our minds or that battle of negative thoughts and unregulated feelings can consume us.

MAPPING A BATTLE STRATEGY

When I (Marcus) was in my mid-thirties, I became the pastor of a community church in Carmel, Indiana. My first week on the job we got the terrible news that a young man had died in a tragic car crash. He was wrapping up a trip with a group of friends when the vehicle blew a tire at high speed and flipped several times. Some had survived, but some—like this young man—had died. It was an agonizing event on several levels. One of the first things I had to do as a pastor was sit down with this young man's mother and his fiancée to process what happened. I had no idea what to say to bring comfort at a time like this. The young man had just graduated from college and was planning to marry his fiancée that summer before starting med school. In a horrifying instant, what appeared to be a charmed life crashed into unrecognizable oblivion.

The fiancée did not live in the area, so we only met a few times, but the mother was a member of the church and we met more regularly. One of the assignments I eventually gave her was to start each day with a journaling exercise. As someone who has experienced both the reality of God and the reality of the devil many times, and because she was coming to me for pastoral care, I asked her to start with two questions. (1) What lie is the devil trying to get me to believe today? (2) What is the truth God wants me to hold on to instead? Each week she would share her journaling with me. A few years later, I received an email from her thanking me for the journaling exercise with the comment, "It probably saved my life."

Part of turning your brain into an anteater is preparing a battle strategy. This means you want to be equipped, and we recommend you start with the seven core upsetting emotions we looked at in chapter 6. When we do not stay ourselves and return to joy from each emotion, they quickly become toxic motivators we use to motivate ourselves or others in some way. Dr. Wilder has identified these as the big six negative emotions that get triggered by attachment issues. The seventh is attachment pain, the pain of loss, which is what the woman who lost her son was feeling intensely. Here is a quick summary:

- Sadness—the feeling that I have lost what brought me joy.
- Anger—the high-energy feeling that makes me want to destroy something or stop what is causing me pain or creating injustice.

- Disgust—the feeling that I want to vomit because something feels toxic and I just need to get away from it.
- Shame—the feeling that I do not bring you joy and you are not happy to see me. Shame tends to make me want to hang my head and avoid eye contact.
- Fear—the high-energy feeling that makes me want to run away from danger.
- Despair—the low-energy feeling that comes from realizing that fixing my problem is impossible—that I lack the time and resources to make things better.
- Attachment pain—the deep inner pain that comes from not being able to connect with someone who brings you joy. They may be out of town, or shut down emotionally, or unavailable for some other reason, but there is pain inside because that connection is unavailable.

Of course, these are not the only negative emotions that exist. However, most of the other names we give to emotions can be understood as various levels of these emotions or various combinations of these emotions. For example, disappointment may be a combination of disgust, despair, and sadness. Annoyance is low-level anger. Rage is high-level anger. It is not uncommon for people to have several negative emotions happening at the same time.

Choose one of these emotions and make a list of common thoughts that often support it. If you struggle with despair, make a list of thoughts that feel true when hopelessness is creeping in. One man who did this exercise made a list something like this.

1. Unemployment is death.
2. I am doomed.
3. There is no way out of this mess.
4. I am a failure.
5. I have no future.

Once you have identified the most common thoughts that attack you when you feel this particular emotion, begin making a list of replacement thoughts you will think instead.

1. The future is not yet written.
2. Unexpected reversals for the good often happen.
3. I can make a plan.
4. I am not alone. I can seek help.

The goal is to learn to recognize common attacks in our thought life and prepare ourselves to replace those thoughts with ones that are more helpful.

"SOMETHING DARKER THAN THE DARKNESS"

At the beginning of the chapter we alluded to the idea that we are not unfamiliar with either God or the devil.

Both of us are convinced that there is a real darkness in this world that is personal and not simply biological. We could share hundreds of stories to support this, but let us offer one example here.

A young man I (Marcus) know struggled with depression for years and was desperate to get help. He read some of my other books and was attending one of my training events. At a break, he asked if there was any way we could meet before I left the city. I had a friend with me who was very experienced with inner battles and the two of us agreed to meet with the young man. He told us that when he was thirteen he had gone into a depression and moved into his attic. He had put up dark curtains and was determined to live in darkness. However, he said, "One day, something darker than the darkness moved in and I have never been able to get rid of it."

That day my friend and I led him through a process I describe in a few of my other books that address spiritual warfare.[3] At one point we led him to make a declaration, "This is not a battle between me and you. This is a battle between you and Christ. I command you to take your claim against me to the cross." The young man had barely finished these words when he started to weep with one of the most gut-wrenching cries I have ever heard. After a few moments, he said over and over again, "It's gone. It's gone. I can't believe it's finally gone." The tears continued to flow.

A few years later, I saw that young man again and hardly recognized him. He had put on muscle, he was smiling and engaging and playful with his wife and young children. He pulled me aside and said, "I just want you to know I haven't had a day of depression since I saw you last. Something really broke."

We don't tell this story to suggest that all deep problems have a simple solution, but to point out that part of what is going on with "unwinnable" battles in our minds involves real spiritual darkness. We have found that spiritual problems are not resolved by human solutions. Spiritual battles require spiritual strategies.

SO, WHAT ABOUT RELIGION?

Does it matter whether I am Christian or Muslim or Buddhist or atheist or something else when it comes to joy? The simple answer is no. You can increase your joy regardless of your faith or your worldview. The differences between our faiths have more to do with how well they explain reality. As Christians, Chris and I are convinced it helps to have a relationship with a God who is happy to see us and happy to go through suffering with us because it means we are never alone. It also helps to have a community of people who support each other in hard times. But the reality is that when it comes to joy, anyone with positive relationships and a positive attitude has access to this important emotion. This is a surprise to some Christians who believe the Holy Spirit is the only source of true joy, but we have met with many friends who embrace other views of reality and yet experience real joy.

Having said this, there is a universal angst most people experience as they look for a way to fill the longing in their hearts. Many of these people experience joy now and then but know there is still something missing. We have seen many people searching for an answer to this longing find what they were looking for in a relationship with Jesus. From this perspective, the worldview of Christianity is especially suited to help people live with joy and peace. It offers a solution to shame through the forgiveness of sin. It offers a solution to the fear of death through the promise of eternal life. It offers hope in times of despair and a God whose love cannot be measured.

COMPLETING OUR JOY HOUSE

So far in this book we have looked at how to build a foundation for joy by learning to practice calming and appreciation. Then we explored how to build a framework for the house by learning to tell stories that help us create a narrative of hope around the big emotions in life. In this chapter, we looked at how to complete the house by gaining some skills in how to attack toxic thoughts.

As we wrap up the book in our final chapter, we want to talk about how to fill our joy house with good things by learning to build healthy habits over the course of our lives. The goal is to look back at the end of life and see that we have lived with joy and learned what satisfies—and in turn, share our joy with others.

JOY WORKOUTS FOR ATTACKING TOXIC THOUGHTS

Winning the battle for our minds is not always a simple, straightforward process. However, we think you will find some help by practicing the four exercises included here.

JOY WORKOUT #11—*Finding faulty beliefs*

We now practice an exercise that combines a number of skills. First, we identify some of the faulty beliefs that carry weight in our lives. Next, we notice how these feel in our body and we try to identify emotions that may be attached to these beliefs. We explore qualities we like about ourselves and try to discover what positive traits these beliefs say about who we are. This exercise requires a good mixture of vulnerability with some gentleness for our tender places.

1. Use your phone or journal to write out some of the faulty beliefs that come to mind for the following categories. These are beliefs you would like to update and replace. You can pick one or two of the following options or review all five if you have time.

   a. List general beliefs about yourself, your value, and your self-worth that you would like to change:

      i. Include what each belief feels like in your body.

      ii. Include any feelings or emotions that go with these beliefs.

      iii. Include statements about what you like about yourself that you wouldn't want to change.

      iv. Can you see any positive trait that these beliefs or fears say about you? What kind of person would be bothered by what bothers you?

         For example, if I fear messing up all the time, the positive is that I am someone who values doing a good job at whatever

I do. So, the positive attribute is that I care deeply about who I am and what I do.

b. Beliefs about your looks and appearance:

   i. Include what each belief feels like in your body.

   ii. Include any feelings or emotions that go with these beliefs.

   iii. Include statements about what you like about yourself that you wouldn't want to change.

   iv. Can you see any positive trait that these beliefs or fears say about you? What kind of person would be bothered by what bothers you?

c. Beliefs about your past successes or failures:

   i. Include what each belief feels like in your body.

   ii. Include any feelings or emotions that go with these beliefs.

   iii. Include statements about what you like about yourself that you wouldn't want to change.

   iv. Can you see any positive trait that these beliefs or fears say about you? What kind of person would be bothered by what bothers you?

d. Beliefs about your future and legacy:

      i. Include what each belief feels like in your body.

      ii. Include any feelings or emotions that go with these beliefs.

      iii. Include statements about what you like about yourself that you wouldn't want to change.

      iv. Can you see any positive trait that these beliefs or fears say about you? What kind of person would be bothered by what bothers you?

   e. Common beliefs or fears that rob your joy on a regular basis:

      i. Include what each belief feels like in your body.

      ii. Include any feelings or emotions that go with these beliefs.

      iii. Include statements about what you like about yourself that you wouldn't want to change.

      iv. Can you see any positive trait that these beliefs or fears say about you? What kind of person would be bothered by what bothers you?

2. Set a timer for three minutes and practice calming and quieting. You can think about something positive like a recent joy moment if you like.

3. Think about a time you helped someone or did something kind. What values or qualities are present in this scenario?

4. Think about a time you were generous toward another person. What values or qualities are present in this scenario?

JOY WORKOUT #12—*The gift of appreciation*

We explore receiving feedback from others "outside of ourselves" to see if we can influence our faulty beliefs. It can feel difficult to receive appreciation and joy from other people. This is a good opportunity to receive and give the gift of appreciation.

1. As you reflect on some of your faulty beliefs from the previous exercise, can you find any "evidence" or experiences that reinforces these thoughts? For example, I may believe that I will never amount to anything useful or good. I can say, "Well, it's no accident that I believe this! It's what my father used to say to me all the time . . ."

2. Our brain's identity center sees itself by how we perceive others see us. Here is where joy enters the picture. We see ourselves in the reflection of a face that lights up to see us. Getting feedback from people who love us can instill confidence and update our minds with a different perspective. Try the following

steps with people you trust because this section requires a level of vulnerability.

   a. Invite people you know and trust to tell you some of the qualities they enjoy about you.
   b. Ask if they can think of times or scenarios where they observed these qualities in action.
   c. Invite your friend to share a story about a time they saw something in you they admired and respected.

3. Now switch roles. Share with your friend answers to these questions so your friend receives your appreciation and corresponding stories that come to mind.

JOY WORKOUT #13—*Identify toxic motivators*

We now focus on identifying toxic motivators that influence us. We can use these emotions to get results in us and in other people. When we do not return to joy from these feelings, they can drive us and influence our thinking, decision-making, and behavior. If angry, I use the threat of anger to get people to respond in a certain way. Maybe I slam a cabinet door, stomp off, or even use the "silent treatment" to punish loved ones and get a certain response. We look at identifying possible replacements for these motivators and explore how joy and desire-driven motivators could look.

1. Use a journal or phone to discuss where you see toxic motivators impacting your decision-making and relationships.

   a. I use sadness to motivate me or others:
      Instead of sadness, I could use joy in this way:

   b. I use anxiety and fear to motivate me or others:
      Instead of anxiety and fear, I could use joy in this way:

   c. I use disgust to motivate me or others:
      Instead of disgust to motivate, I could use joy in this way:

   d. I use shame to motivate me or others:
      Instead of shame to motivate, I could use joy in this way:

   e. I use anger to motivate me or others:
      Instead of anger to motivate, I could use joy in this way:

   f. I use despair and hopelessness to motivate me and others:
      Instead of despair and hopelessness to motivate, I could use joy in this way:

   g. I use threat of loss and attachment pain to motivate me and others:
      Instead of loss and attachment pain to motivate, I could use joy in this way:

2. If these pockets of your life were fueled by joy instead of unpleasant emotions, what would change for each emotion?

3. Can you think of people you know who use these toxic motivators in some way? What is the response of other people? Where do you see this in other places such as leadership positions and more?

4. Who do you know in your network who handles the SADSAD emotions in such a way that you see they remain relational and recover from their upsets well?

5. If you have a relationship with these people, share what you are learning and invite them to tell you a story about how they learned these skills.

6. If possible, invite the person to tell you a story about a time they successfully recovered from an upset or stayed relational in the midst of the upset.

7. Find a friend or family member to share your thoughts and discoveries from this exercise.

JOY WORKOUT #14—*Gratitude and appreciation*

According to neuroscientist Dr. Andrew D. Huberman, dramatic shifts in mood and neurochemistry come from receiving gratitude as well as when we observe other people enjoying gratitude.[4] Giving, receiving, and observing gratitude produces a deep and meaningful response. Because of the interplay between gratitude, staying relational, and compassion, we can see that people often lose the desire and ability to be compassionate when they lose their joy and their brain's relational circuits start to fade. We now practice using gratitude and appreciation to gauge how compassionate we feel.

1. Identify three things you are thankful for today. Give each a name and identify how you feel reflecting on these things.

2. Identify three things you are thankful for from your month. Give each a name and identify how you feel as you reflect on each highlight.

3. Identify three highlights from your year. Give each a name and identify how you feel as you reflect on each highlight.

4. Notice your level of compassion with the following statements and write out your thoughts.

    a. I feel concern for the sufferings of my family and friends when I see them hurting.

    b. I enjoy seeing people get punished when I feel they deserve it.

    c. It's easy to feel sympathy for people I know.

    d. It's easy for me to feel sympathy for strangers I don't know.

    e. I am glad to be with people who are hurting and suffering.

    f. The conditions where I find it easy to be compassionate are:

    g. The conditions where it is hard to be compassionate are:

5. Find a friend and share your thoughts and practice the exercise together. Discuss how your answers might change if you were having a bad day today instead of practicing gratitude.

CHAPTER 8

Satisfaction

HAVE YOU EVER SEEN a house on TV or visited someone's home and thought, "I love this place. If I could build my dream house, it would look a lot like this"? It isn't just that the house is expensive. It reflects something about your heart. I (Marcus) remember visiting a camp one time to see if it would make a nice spot for a retreat. It was in the mountains of Colorado and was decorated with rough-hewn timber, wood floors, leather couches, and a giant fireplace. But that was not all. One side of the room had floor-to-ceiling windows at least two stories tall looking straight at a granite peak covered in snow. You could follow the slope of the mountain from the valley below to the timberline to the majestic granite and get lost in the view. More ridges and peaks could be seen in the distance. It was breathtaking. A large stone patio called to me and I wandered outside to take in the full experience.

To this day, I can visit that spot in my mind and relive the sense of awe and the feeling it created in me. When my daughter was seven, she had a similar experience. We went on a vacation to the ocean. She is from Indiana and had never seen the ocean before. The sight overwhelmed her with wonder. She walked out in the backyard, sat down, and just stared at it for nearly an hour.

Nature often calls to something deep inside of us. Beauty and grandeur, intricacy, and variety—time spent in nature is rarely unsatisfying.

What you find satisfying reveals a great deal about who you are. Our hearts come alive with music, art, athletic endeavors, cooking for dear friends—all kinds of good things. It depends on how we are wired and what we have learned to love. People who don't know what they find satisfying generally struggle to know who they really are. Our identity and our passions are intimately connected.

Too many of us fill our lives with temporary pleasures that don't really satisfy. They are fun for a moment, but even a few hours later the pleasure has faded. It would be nice to fill our lives with trips to the ocean and views of the mountains, but as with joy, the secret to filling our lives with satisfying experiences is not just about the "wow moments" that knock us on our heels and leave us amazed. The secret is to learn to spend our day doing satisfying work and recognizing the little things we can experience on a daily or weekly basis that give us the sense that "this is good."

For most of this book we have focused on the four habits we need to develop in order to build an internal joy house. You can think of this chapter as exploring how to fill that house with good things that increase our sense of satisfaction in life. The key word here is satisfaction. Let's start with a quick look at what that is and why it is so important.

WHAT MAKES AN EXPERIENCE SATISFYING?

My (Marcus) dream as a teenager was to play basketball for my local high school—a powerhouse with one of the best coaches in the state of Indiana. The team won its sectional championship nearly every year. I was an outsider who had attended private school through ninth grade. I didn't know anyone in the basketball program, and no one knew me. My heart sank on the opening day of tryouts when I saw over a hundred young men trying out for the team. I wasn't sure how I would get noticed, let alone how I would impress the coaches enough to make the roster. When the day finally came and they posted the names of the players who had made the cut, mine was the last name on the list (alphabetically "Warner" is often at the end).

Making the team was an amazing feeling. It was also the satisfying result of a lot of hard work. I spent the summer running a three-mile route through the local park several times a week (and I hate running). I used to dribble a ball with my left hand on uneven sidewalks for the mile or so it took to get to school. I played in every pickup basketball game I could find. I ran the stairs in the school gym. I did ball handling drills and shot at least a hundred free throws nearly every day.

My family had done a good job of teaching me that some things are worth working for and waiting for. As a teenager, making the basketball team was one of those things.

So what makes an experience satisfying? Here are a few characteristics that separate the truly satisfying from the merely pleasurable.

Creativity. Hobbies that call out our creativity and allow us to express something of what is in our hearts are always more satisfying than things that are easy and short-lived. One of the traits that characterizes joy-filled people is the habit of filling their lives with creative activity and hobbies that satisfy, which can include:

> Music
> Sports
> Art
> Crafts
> Writing
> Gardening

Relationships. Many activities that we find satisfying are things we do on our own, but that does not mean they are not relational. For example, as I write this book, I am in a room by myself. But I am routinely thinking about my coauthor, my editor, my audience, and people I am hoping will like what I have produced. Part of the joy of writing is hoping it will make someone happy. There is a relational payoff in the end.

Some activities are fun because of the relational connection involved. Several times through the years I took my kids to a Renaissance fair. It was fun for me, but most of the fun was watching how excited my kids got. The feeling I get even now thinking back on those memories is much more satisfying than the many times we have been in the same room but each doing our own thing—one watching a video, another surfing the internet, someone else doing work. It is not the same.

Effort. Satisfying things are worth working for. There is something satisfying about a do-it-yourself project. Making things with your own hands or going through the process of working hard to achieve something, even if it is small, brings a level of satisfaction that doesn't come with experiences that are easy and short-lived.

As a kid, I remember entering art contests and spending hours trying to perfect a portrait for that contest. My mom, who was an artist herself, helped me get the shading just right and showed me how to get the proportions correct. There was a feeling of real satisfaction in stepping back and seeing that the face I had drawn actually looked a lot like the picture on which it was based.

Waiting. Satisfying things are worth waiting for. Gardening is a great example of this. There is a time for preparing the soil, a time for planting the seed, a time for tending the plant, and a time for blooming or harvesting. Knowing there will be beauty or flavor at the end of the process reminds us that the work and the waiting are worth it.

When we don't know what satisfies, we don't know what is worth working for and waiting for. We don't know who we are and how it is like us to act. On the other hand, when we fill our lives with good habits, they reward us with a deep sense of satisfaction.

The joy lasts. Merely pleasurable experiences don't create lasting joy. They are fun in the moment and then they are over. Satisfying experiences create a feeling of pleasure we can revisit again and again. The feeling lasts over time. For instance, I have memories of times at the lake that I can revisit and find myself involuntarily smiling.

Chris and I first started pondering the significance of satisfaction because of the role Dr. Wilder gave it in the process of growing maturity. He taught that parents need to help their children distinguish between what is merely pleasurable for the moment and what brings lasting satisfaction. Children who live for temporary pleasures do not develop maturity, because they do not develop the emotional resilience that allows them to bounce back from hard things. On the other hand, children who learn how to work for and wait for what is good live with a higher level of satisfaction. This process anchors their identity and helps them know how it is like them to act no matter what is going on in life and relationships.

Parents need to help their children distinguish between what is merely pleasurable for the moment and what brings lasting satisfaction.

What will we wish we had spent our lives doing? Having presided at several funerals and having walked with those families through the grieving and planning associated with such times, Chris and I have often been struck with the way death puts life into perspective. On such occasions, I have often shared the words of an ancient text in Ecclesiastes 7:2: "It is better to go to a house of mourning than to go to a house of feasting, since that is the end of all mankind, and the living should take it to heart."

It may seem odd in a book on joy to talk about death. But joy is not meant to be an escape from reality. It is part of what gives our short lives meaning. The primary speaker in Ecclesiastes reflects on this and says, "So I commend the enjoyment of life, because there is nothing better for a person under the sun than to eat and drink and be glad. Then joy will accompany them in their toil all the days of the life God has given them under the sun" (Eccl. 8:15 NIV).

In Ecclesiastes, the phrase "life under the sun" stands in contrast to eternity. The entire book is, in many ways, an ode to the meaninglessness of life if there is no eternity. The term "life under the sun" reminds us that this life is short and nothing is guaranteed. The book also reflects on the idea that God has set eternity in our hearts so that we long not just for joy in this life, but for the hope of something eternal. We can take all of the characteristics of satisfaction listed above and, when we think about them in light of eternity, they simply grow more profound.

I remember one particular funeral. As I watched a slide show of highlights of the man's life, I realized that all of the pictures were of family or friends and of the memorable moments they shared. It was also clear that this person loved the water. The family spent a lot of time at the lake. It hit me in a memorable way that life is short and we want to fill it with things that matter. For most of us, that means the joy we share with people we love and the satisfaction of investing in work that makes a difference to others.

HOW HABITS GROW

The brain science behind the development of habits is complex but the essentials are relatively straightforward.

Repetitive activity links neurons in the brain so that neuron pathways begin to form. These pathways allow us to do common tasks more quickly because there is already a linked connection related to that task. As the habit grows, the neural pathways related to that habit begin to get wrapped in white matter. The brain is incredibly fast at processing information. Gray matter can process data at up to six cycles per second. White matter, however, is super fast. It can process data at up to two hundred cycles per second. Finding white matter in the brain is generally a sign that a strong habit has been formed.

The problem with white matter is that it will form just as predictably around bad habits as good habits. It can form around thought patterns (like positive or negative self-talk) as well as activities (like typing or riding a bike). If we develop bad habits in the way we think, those negative thoughts will run our lives. The only way to overcome a bad habit is to build a good one to take its place. In a sense, life consists of the habits we develop, so it is worth taking the time to do the exercises in this book in order to build habits that transform our lives from the inside out.

The good news when it comes to habits is that it is almost never too late to grow them. The brain is capable of building neural pathways and forming white matter for as long as we live (unless there is something physically wrong preventing this). The more scientists learn about neuroplasticity, the more we realize how important it is to develop new habits.

JEN LEARNS NEW RELATIONAL HABITS

We mentioned Chris's wife, Jen, in chapter 1. When they first met, it was a good day when Jen got out of bed. As Chris and Jen began practicing brain-based habits like joy and rest, everything changed. The joy practice certainly transformed Jen's life. However, one skill in particular changed life as she knew it—the skill of resting, calming, and quieting. Jen saw the world in a new light. She started to feel peaceful. She felt refreshed instead of anxious and exhausted for the first time she could remember. Jen's mind, feelings, thoughts, and motivation were renovated in new ways. Jen felt alive!

Because Jen never learned the habit of calming, she avoided rest states. This meant high-energy joy was easy, but low-energy rest was not. Because Jen never learned this habit, something else grew in its place. We can call it the weed of pseudo-rest, which meant Jen's idea of resting in college was watching television while she ate dinner and graded calculus papers. Imagine this approach to resting!

Since Jen did not rest, this meant she went to bed exhausted and pretty much collapsed at the end of each day. Collapsing at the end of the day was how Jen compensated for the lack of rest and quiet.

Jen was part of the practice group Chris was running at the organization where he worked. The group would slowly and methodically practice learning new relational skills, many of them mentioned in this book.[1] For resting, Chris would set a timer for thirty seconds and give the group practice to see if they could rest. People sat in their seats while Chris invited the group to be still and try to quiet their minds and bodies while they took deep breaths. At first, everyone hated this! Most complained that it was too long, too boring, and too ridiculous. Thirty seconds may not sound like much to us, but for the group who didn't have this habit, the practice felt difficult, even tormenting.

Eventually, the group worked their way up to three minutes for resting and quieting. Over time, it increased to five minutes. As Jen continued practicing this new habit, her brain started to learn how to calm down, and feel refreshed. Soon, she started craving rest and quiet times. Jen's brain was learning this new habit, and the old ways of avoiding rest started to disappear. If you met Jen today, you would never know there was a time she didn't have this skill!

Jen is now a leader who trains people to learn the skills she once did not have. Learning new skills and strengthening existing skills has increased the satisfaction levels in Jen's life. "I never knew this much joy and peace was possible!" she now says. "I'm no longer a walking, talking ball of tension. I have peace. I feel calm. I have hope."

As you have read through this book, our guess is that you have done some self-examination. Most of us know there is a gap between the level of joy we experience and the level of joy we desire. The good news is there are exercises included in this book that have a proven track record of helping people grow their joy. As you do these exercises and develop the four habits of joy-filled people, your emotional capacity will start to grow.

We all need to pay attention to the kind of house we build in our inner world. If we succeed in building a joy house and filling it with satisfying experiences, our inner world becomes a safe, stable place to be. Too many of us live with a fear house in our inner world, and it is sucking the life out of us. We didn't build a fear house on purpose. We just didn't get the help we needed to build something different.

Our hope is that the four habits described in this book will give you the blueprint you need to build the joy house you have always wanted.

A FINAL NOTE

As Christians, we believe God wired us for joy and that He desires to share joy with us. Jesus said, "I have told you these things so that my joy may be in you and your joy may be complete" (John 15:11 csb). In Numbers 6:24–26, we read that every day the high priest of Israel was to pray this blessing on his people, "May the Lord bless you and keep you. May the Lord cause His face to shine upon you and be gracious to you. May the Lord lift His face to you and give you peace." If you think about it, when someone's face "shines" upon us, it is because they are happy to see us. When someone "lifts their face toward us" it means they see us and are happy to be with us. This is our hope for you too.

ACKNOWLEDGMENTS

BOTH OF US GOT STARTED on this journey of understanding joy and the brain and its crucial role in life because of the influence of Dr. Jim Wilder, so we want to thank him for the pioneering work he did and the personal help he has continued to offer. We also want to acknowledge the role our friends at Northfield have played in encouraging us to get these concepts into writing. We are specifically grateful for the many hours Betsey Newenhuyse put into improving this book and making sure it was ready for the public!

NOTES

INTRODUCTION

1. Andrew Steptoe et al., "Neuroendocrine and Inflammatory Factors Associated with Positive Affect in Healthy Men and Women: The Whitehall II Study," *American Journal of Epidemiology* 167, no. 1 (January 2008), https://doi.org/10.1093/aje/kwm252.

2. Ruth Buczynski, PhD, and Dan Siegel, MD, "The Neurobiology of Trauma," *National Institute for the Clinical Application of Behavioral Health* (October 2017): 21–22. Neurobiology tells us what we do with our minds can alter the molecules of our health. Telomeres are part of our DNA strands, which decrease with age and stress. The best predictors for how these strands are optimized comes down to what we do with our mind.

CHAPTER 1: JOY, TRAUMA, AND BUILDING OUR HOUSE

1. E. James Wilder et al., *Living from the Heart Jesus Gave You* (East Peoria, IL: Shepherd's House, Inc., 2013), 83–89.

2. Learn more about THRIVE Training at thrivetoday.org.

3. The work of developmental neuropsychologist Dr. Allan Schore from UCLA says regulating high-energy states (joy)

to sharing low-energy states (rest) are the best predictors for lifelong mental health.

4. Corrie ten Boom, *The Hiding Place* (Grand Rapids: Chosen Books, 2006), 220.

5. Genes and experience have a close partnership. Genes do not act apart from experience, which determines when and how genes express themselves over time. Maturation of the brain is experience-dependent and heavily influenced by caregiver reactions. Allan Schore, "Early Organization of the Nonlinear Right Brain and Development of a Predisposition to Psychiatric Disorders," *Development and Psychopathology* 9, no. 4 (1997): 595–631; Schore, *Affect Regulation and the Origin of the Self: The Neurobiology of Emotional Development* (Hillsdale, NJ: Lawrence Erlbaum Associates Publishers, 1994), 9–20.

6. The brain's "joy center" is the right-hemisphere orbital prefrontal cortex, which reaches its peak between eight and ten months of life and is impacted by early social experiences. Schore, *Affect Regulation and the Origin of the Self*; Schore, "The Experience-Dependent Maturation of an Evaluative System in the Cortex," in K. Pribram, ed., *Brain and Values: Is a Biological Science of Values Possible?* (Mahweh, NJ: Lawrence Erlbaum Associates Publishers, 1998), 337–58.

7. Schore, *Affect Regulation and the Origin of the Self*.

8. The relational right hemisphere is dominant in preverbal human infants, and indeed for the first three years of life. Allan Schore, "Attachment and the Regulation of the Right Brain," *Attachment & Human Development* 2, no. 1 (April 2000): 23–47.

CHAPTER 2: THE BRAIN SCIENCE OF JOY

1. Visit "Morejoy Harvard" at https://hwpi.harvard.edu/ morejoy/cultivate-joy-at-work.

2. Visit the following link for the Yale Center for Faith & Culture at Yale Divinity School: https://faith.yale.edu/ legacy-projects/theology-of-joy.

3. fMRI technology was developed around 1991 and tracked blood flow in the brain so that it became possible to see which parts of the brain "lit up" during various tasks and emotions.

4. Dr. Allan Schore is on the clinical faculty of the Department of Psychiatry and Biobehavioral Sciences and UCLA David Geffen School of Medicine. He is author of six seminal volumes, *Affect Regulation and the Origin of the Self*, *Affect Dysregulation and Disorders of the Self*, *Affect Regulation and the Repair of the Self*, *The Science of the Art of Psychotherapy*, *Right Brain Psychotherapy*, and *The Development of the Unconscious Mind*, as well as numerous articles and chapters. His Regulation Theory, grounded in developmental neuroscience and developmental psychoanalysis, focuses on the origin, psychopathogenesis, and psychotherapeutic treatment of the early forming subjective implicit self: www .allanschore.com.

5. The expression "Einstein of psychoanalysis" can be found in an article titled "An Interview with Dr. Allan Schore" in *The Science of Psychotherapy*, July 14, 2014, https://www.thescience ofpsychotherapy.com/an-interview-with-allan-schore.

6. "Allan Schore: Joy & Fun," YouTube, July 11, 2011, https:// www.youtube.com/watch?v=Y0iocZu1mVg.

7. These influencers include people like Daniel Siegel, Daniel Amen, Bessel van der Kolk, Antonio DaMasio, and Iain McGilchrist, to name a few.

8. Jeffrey Kluger, "The Power of Joy," *Time*, November 13, 2020.

9. E. James Wilder et al., *Joy Starts Here: The Transformation Zone* (East Peoria, IL: Shepherd's House, Inc., 2013), 237.

10. In his many works, Dr. Schore placed a bright spotlight on research that demonstrates infants respond with joy when they see the "sparkle" on the mother's face in response to seeing the child. The joyful responses between parents and children form a foundational element of attachment theory. Schore says that infants and mothers are "psychobiologically" attuned as both of their right hemispheres connect through eye contact. Allan Schore, *Affect Regulation and the Origin of the Self: The Neurobiology of Emotional Development* (Hillsdale, NJ: Lawrence Erlbaum Associates Publishers, 1994), 76.

11. Schore, *Affect Regulation and the Origin of the Self*, 136. Schore states the emotionally expressive face of the imprinting object stimulates infant opioid production as part of the attachment process. In mutual face-gazing experiences, the mother's face activates high levels of endogenous opiates, natural opioids, in her infant. H. S. Hoffman, "Imprinting and the Critical period for Social Attachments: Some Laboratory Investigations," in M. H. Bornstein, ed., *Sensitive Periods in Development: Interdisciplinary Studies* (Hillsdale, NJ: Lawrence Erlbaum Associates Publishers), 99–121.

12. Ibid.

13. Susan Kuchinskas, *The Chemistry of Connection: How the Oxytocin Response Can Help You Find Trust, Intimacy, and Love* (Oakland, CA: New Harbinger Publications, 2009), 12–14.

14. Ibid., 2.

15. Brady Wilson, "The Big Release: 3 Brain Hacks to Give You Brilliance on Demand," Inc., May 31, 2016, https://www.inc.com/brady-wilson/the-big-release-3-brain-hacks-to-give-you-brilliance-on-demand.html.

16. These concepts are introduced in E. James Wilder et al., *Living from the Heart Jesus Gave You* (East Peoria, IL: Shepherd's House, Inc., 2013).

17. The prefrontal cortex, which has two subdivisions, the orbitofrontal and dorsolateral cortices, make up 30 percent of the total cortical mass of the human brain. Schore, *Affect Regulation and the Origin of the Self*, 42.

18. Wilder, et al., *Living from the Heart Jesus Gave You*, 83–89.

19. The infant-mother mutual gaze interactions, or "affect synchrony," start around two months and provide the opportunity for a number of brain areas and skills to develop. Schore, *Affect Regulation and the Repair of The Self*, 113–22.

20. Allan Schore, *Affect Dysregulation and Disorders of the Self* (New York: W. W. Norton & Company, 2003), 112–115; Wilder, et al., *Living from the Heart Jesus Gave You*, 78.

21. Wilder et al., *Living from the Heart Jesus Gave You*, 74–81.

22. Marcus Warner and Chris M. Coursey, *The 4 Habits of Joy-Filled Marriages* (Chicago: Northfield Publishing, 2019).

CHAPTER 3: CALMING: HABIT #1

1. Search YouTube for "Shalom My Body," or use this link: https://bit.ly/39PNH79.

2. Marcus Warner and Stefanie Hinman, *Building Bounce: How to Grow Emotional Resilience* (Carmel, IN: Deeper Walk International, 2020).

3. A portion of this exchange and others is available on the "Chris Coursey—THRIVEtoday" YouTube channel. The video is called "Return to Joy from Fear Training."

4. Learn more about getting our relational footing in emotions in Chris Coursey, *The Joy Switch: How Your Brain's Secret Circuit Affects Your Relationships—And How You Can Activate It* (Chicago: Northfield Publishers, 2021).

5. Two "Shalom My Body" videos are posted on the "Chris Coursey—THRIVEtoday" YouTube page: "The Joy Switch: Shalom My Body" and "Shalom My Body Exercises."

CHAPTER 4: APPRECIATING: HABIT #2

1. Liz Mineo, "Good Genes Are Nice, but Joy Is Better," Harvard Gazette, April 11, 2017, https://news.harvard.edu/gazette/story/2017/04/over-nearly-80-years-harvard-study-has-been-showing-how-to-live-a-healthy-and-happy-life.

2. This Harvard study has spent over seventy-five years tracking 724 men, while sixty are still alive into their nineties. The study continues to follow the participants' more than two thousand children. Robert Waldinger, "What Makes a Good Life? Lessons from the Longest Study on Happiness," YouTube, January 25, 2016, https://www.youtube.com/watch?v=8KkKuTCFvzI.

3. Mineo, "Good Genes Are Nice, but Joy Is Better."

4. For a summary of this TED Talk and interview with the director of the study, Robert Waldinger, visit adultdevelopment study.org.

5. Ibid.

6. The work of developmental neuropsychologist Dr. Allan Schore says regulating high-energy states (joy) to sharing low-energy states (rest) are the best predictors for lifelong mental health.

CHAPTER 6: MATURITY AND THE BIG SIX PROTECTOR EMOTIONS

1. These maturity stages are based on the Life Model and the work of Dr. Jim Wilder.

2. Learn more at lifemodelworks.org.

3. Sue Gerhardt, "The Power of a Smile," The Natural Child Project, https://www.naturalchild.org/articles/guest/sue_gerhardt.html.

4. Manas K. Mandal and Nalini Ambady, "Laterality of Facial Expressions of Emotion: Universal and Culture-Specific Influences," *Behavioural Neurology* 15 (2004): 23–34, https://doi.org/10.1155/2004/786529.

5. Allan Schore, "A Neuropsychoanalytic Viewpoint: Commentary on Paper by Steven H. Knoblauch," *Psychoanalytic Dialogues* 15, no. 6 (2005): 829–54, https://www.allanschore.com/pdf/SchorePsychoanalyticDial05.pdf.

6. Bill Atwood, *The General, The Boy, and Recapturing Joy* (Frisco, TX: Ekklesia Society Publishing, 2020), 67.

7. This story is included in Chris Coursey, *The Joy Switch: How Your Brain's Secret Circuit Affects Your Relationships—And How You Can Activate It* (Chicago: Northfield Publishing, 2021).

CHAPTER 7: ATTACK TOXIC THOUGHTS: HABIT #4

1. Daniel G. Amen and Mike Marino, *Feel Better Fast: Learn How to Think Positive & Kill the ANTs That Ruin Your Happiness* (A.C.I. Clinical Audio Series, 2005).

2. Daniel Amen, "Do You Have an ANT Infestation in Your Head?," Amen Clinics, September 16, 2020, https://www.amenclinics.com/blog/do-you-have-an-ant-infestation-in-your-head/.

3. See Marcus Warner, *Understanding the Wounded Heart* and *What Every Believer Should Know About Spiritual Warfare*.

4. Andrew Huberman, "The Science of Gratitude & How to Build a Gratitude Practice | Huberman Lab Podcast #47," YouTube video, November 22, 2021, https://www.youtube.com/watch?v=KVjfFN89qvQ.

CHAPTER 8: SATISFACTION

1. All nineteen relational skills can be found at thrivetoday.org. See also Chris Coursey, *Transforming Fellowship: 19 Brain Skills That Build Joyful Community* (Coursey Creations, LLC, 2022).

THRIVEtoday

So many people feel stuck. They want more out of life and relationships but feel like they are missing something. All too often, what's absent for many people are important relational skills! **Chris and his wife, Jen, work alongside a dedicated team passionate about leading joy-filled lives.**

THRIVEtoday is a nonprofit organization that trains individuals, families, and communities in the nineteen relational skills that transform relationships. For over twenty years, the Courseys have been equipping people with joy-oriented character skills so people thrive. When properly trained, the human brain is a beautiful expression of connection and resilience. A healthy brain effects our relationships, improves our lives, furthers our growth, and creates joyful communities that change the world. **THRIVEtoday** offers online events, in-person trainings, and more resources so small groups, individuals, couples, and communities acquire and spread relational skills. Character is cultivated by interactions with people in states of joy and rest. At **THRIVEtoday**, we believe relationships are what life is all about!

Learn more at **thrivetoday.org**.

Take your next step.

Resources & Training in
Heart-Focused Discipleship

Visit our website today for free resources:
deeperwalkinternational.org.